Judith
&
Jim

DRAWN TO MARVEL:
POEMS FROM THE COMIC BOOKS

Published by Minor Arcana Press, Seattle, WA
www.minorarcanapress.com
ISBN: 978-0-9912596-0-1

Library of Congress Control Number: 2014932436

Minor Arcana Press Editor-in-Chief Evan J. Peterson
Cover art by Kelly McQuain
Cover colors and typography by Anne Bean
Interior design and layout by Anne Bean

The interior text is set in Palatino. Titles are set in Dash Decent, a ComicCraft font.

DRAWN TO MARVEL:
POEMS FROM THE COMIC BOOKS

EDITED BY

BRYAN D. DIETRICH AND MARTA FERGUSON

N

A MINOR ARCANA PRESS INCANTATION

We dedicate the following volume to readers, writers, artists, colorists, and designers of both poems and comic books. To all of our contributors and to those submitters not chosen. To the friends and families who have nurtured us during the work of the book and who have let us yammer about this project for the last decade. And most especially, to the three contributors who are no longer here to rejoice with us that the book is *finally* in print. Rest in peace, Kurt Brown, Lucille Clifton, and John Rodriguez.

—*B.D.D. & M.F.*

TABLE OF CONTENTS

EXCELSIOR!

DOOMED... DOOMED!

OH, NO! I'M SWOONING!

IN THE GUTTER

Hold On! I'm Having a Thought!

Beyond the Page

NEW RECRUITS

THE BRONZE AGE

How to Draw Comics

All contributor biographies can be found at
www.minorarcanapress.com.

Foreword

THE ADVENTURES OF THE MEME

I hate be the one to tell you this—and I'll try to do it gently—but… superheroes don't really exist. Not *really*. Not in the one-could-knock-on-your-door-right-now-as-you're-reading-this sense.

And yet they're everywhere, these days, as if their prevalence could make them more actual. The role model might be the church-on-every-corner mentality, crucifix necklaces, "Have a bless' day"…enough of this by the zillionfold, and maybe He *will* be knocking on your door tonight. As might Wonder Woman or Iron Man or, hell, for all I know, Bulletman with his ammo-pointy headgear, if their ubiquity in the worlds of page and screen and molded plastic allow them to cross the threshold of critical mass, and finally become—like Pinocchio, on the other side of his arboreal transformation—"a real boy."

They're ubiquitous, and so is the web of creation and commerce we understand now: the box office returns, the copyright status, the batteries of lawyers, the series spinoffs, the creators' territorial wars, the McToy designers. It seems a more innocent time, when I was twelve and My First Ever Published Work appeared, a letter in *Green Lantern* number 3, Nov-Dec 1960. I couldn't have told you who scripted those stories, or drew them, and I'm not sure how clearly I understood they *were* scripted and drawn, as opposed to somehow simply beamed in purity into this universe, out of a better one (perhaps like the way some people can read the Bible without considering the all-too-human needs behind it?).

And yet in *his* poem here, Ned Balbo knows to honor *Flash* scripter Gardner Fox by name, and to honor his superheroic word production; in a way, the poem is more Fox's than Flash's. Most of the poets here understand the ancestry and the collateral branches of current superherodom: Gilgamesh, Hercules, Jesus, Ishtar, all of those well-intentioned bodhisattvas, on up through the protosuperheroes, Zorro, the Phantom, the Spirit, Doc Savage…. They understand Wonder Woman's place in a talk on queer theory at the MLA, Batman's use by a panel at the AWP convention. Many comic cons and fan blogs and Macy's Thanksgiving balloons and billion-petro-dollar deals away from my letter of 1960, these poems come to us with a richness of cultural infrastructures that Gardner Fox (and Shuster and Siegel, and Kirby) couldn't have guessed at, in their wildest bullpen musings. (They could foresee a spaceship zooming out of the galaxy; they couldn't predict CGI and jargon-smug academic papers.)

And even so—even now that we know the global industry that attends to these characters—some of these poems are so *personally* felt. (When we scowl, there's a "cowl" inside; when we dream of escape, there's a "cape" within.) One's favored superheroes become a lifetime's inspiring touchstones, as they do so overtly in Sherman Alexie's excerpt from *Totem Sonnets*. They become our avatars, our chosen representatives, as the Hulk does, booming his Hulktalk in Greg Santos's poem. They speak for our own outsiderness and aloneness (Michael Martone's The Thing: "...I am another other. And I am on the lookout for other others like me."—or, as Lucille Clifton says to Superman, "there is no planet stranger / than the one I'm from."). And of course, again and again, they embody (in superbodies!) our aspiration toward greatness, a "higher / self descending to inhabit me" (Michael Kriesel).

With a few exceptions (John Ashbery's witty Popeye poem—a Poppaean?—comes to mind), my own contribution, "Powers," must be one of the earliest of this collection, written in 1986-87 and first published in book form in 1990...over a quarter of a century ago! I'm struck by how its language and its sensibility and its emotional tenor echo so obviously in so many of these more recent pieces. By now, it seems, our superheroes aren't simply allusions—they've become memes that we live among. (Gratuitous prediction: in the next ten years there will be a superhero called The Meme.) Okay, maybe they *won't* be knocking at our doors. But clearly they're knocking at our consciousness.

—Albert Goldbarth

Editor's Note

THE DRAWN TO MARVEL STORY

Welcome!

Thank you for picking up this copy of *Drawn to Marvel: Poems from the Comic Books* and bothering to look at the front matter. Maybe you're reading this for class or maybe you've just walked away from one of our regional readings and still have these poems echoing in your head. Maybe you're even one of our submitters or contributors. Maybe you're just curious about why anybody would want to do anthology of superhero poems.

I could make this really short and say: *Because of awesome.* But that doesn't quite cover it. So I'll play project archivist instead.

In 2002, I was the poetry editor at *The Missouri Review*, and I had the real pleasure of accepting Nicholas Allen Harp's "X-Men" for the magazine. The next year, we took some work from Bryan D. Dietrich, also superhero themed. The three of us began to talk. Nick left the country on a Fulbright and Bryan and I continued to talk. In 2009, we started to talk to Chad Parmenter, who chaired an AWP panel, *Poetry and Comix*, featuring Tony Barnstone, Stephen Burt, A. Van Jordan, and Bryan D. Dietrich. Evan J. Peterson, who would later accept the book for Minor Arcana Press, attended that panel and sent us a handful of poems. We started talking to him. This anthology is the product of more than a decade of such conversations.

That whole time, Bryan and I were also writing superhero poems, collecting work, and eventually sending out the anthology, at about half its current length, for publishers to consider. We harangued lots of friends who had done anthologies, asked lots of bothersome technical and financial questions. I want to single out the recently deceased Kurt Brown as having been immensely patient with my questions and generous enough that after the 2009 AWP panel, he gave us more than a dozen poems he'd collected on superhero comics, rather than set up a rival anthology. We are immensely grateful for his help and that of many, many others.

In 2013, we held an open call, but not anticipating we'd get much feedback, we solicited work from a couple dozen writers as well. The overwhelmingly enthusiastic responses to both efforts doubled the size of the book.

As I look back at this note, I realize, I've been giving you the *how* of the book but not the *why*. I think that's because the why is obvious every time somebody grins when I tell them what I'm working on. Comic books are fun. Talking about comic books is fun. Reading and writing about superheroes, supervillains, and monsters? Fun, fun, fun. Pulling together an anthology of same? Super. Fun.

—Marta Ferguson

Introduction

FROM "A DEFENSE OF SUPERHERO POETRY"

Those who write about myth, in any form, are serving "the power seated on the throne of their own soul." Myth can only serve the soul, the soul of humanity. Writing about it, even when it wears tights, also serves that greater soul. How, then, does superhero poetry serve this function? It reinvests us, our world, and our Overstory with wonder. Today's superhero poetry, like the best superhero archetypes themselves, takes one of four tacks to draw us back to marvel. Poems in this genre return wonder to the world by making the mundane super. They return wonder to the world by making the super mundane. They return wonder to modern myths by reviving the superhero, reconnecting the latter to its ancient origins. And finally, they return wonder to the very *tradition* of the mythic by reconnecting us to the sublime, to the Romantic even, through a "pop" back door.

Let us begin with the first, making the mundane super. Ostensibly autobiographical, Albert Goldbarth's poem "Powers" opens with a short catalog of little-remembered, second-tier, Golden Age heroes only the most obsessed geeks would remember: Whizzer, The Top, Phantasmo. He goes on to list others later in the poem—The Streak, Mistress Miracle, Captain Invincible, The Dynamo, Spectral Boy, Silver Comet, The Rocket Avenger, Celestia—but interrupts his exercise in nostalgia with story, the story of his father and himself during the time that, as a child, he would have been reading comics who starred such heroes. The young "Albie," as his father calls him, reverences these super beings, wants to escape his and his family's far more mundane life of bills and talc and "early morning stubble," of "scrappy peddler's stratagems" and "factory outlet jackets," of double shifts and doctor's bills and "every scrap of fiscal scribble that said the rent couldn't be met." The grown voice of the Albie in the poem looks back and imagines himself imagining himself super. After all, The Silver Comet was really "ironically wheelchair-bound and Army-rejected high school student and chemistry ace Lane Barker," and Celestia was "a bosomy ill-paid secretary." The child voice nearly begs, "It could happen—couldn't it?—to me...."

Albie wants his life to be grander, to mean something more, to be larger than the walls of a world where fathers have to scrape by, paycheck to paycheck, their sickly sons reading comics beneath fraying blankets in a cheap apartment with a "bar sign blinking pinkly across the street, the horseshoes of dust" collecting "on the house slippers under the bed," where there is a "sorrily-stained lame angelwing of an ironing board, the ashtrays and the aspirin" populating a life of terrible normalcy, indiscriminate longing. Reading these comics, Albie connects with the idea of "wizard elixirs" and "Wave Transmitter Wristlets, with their wands, their auras, their cowls," and he understands that if he got just one jot of power, real power, "a transfusion of mongoose blood" perhaps, then he could become The Whizzer. If he could strap on a cape, an antigravity belt, develop "bellcurve muscles" and shove them into "blue lamé boots," then he might be able to save himself, save his father, from the shame of the ordinary.

But this is where Goldbarth's poem turns, where it tells us something of the first function of superhero poetry. In calling up the elixir of mongoose blood, he (both young Albie and old) realizes that it is actually his father's blood that "pumps through me, his blood is half of what actually made me" and that it "seems as wondrous as" any blood that might turn him or his father into some half-baked, tri-color, Golden Age comic book hero. In fact, toward the end of the poem, when he watches his father muster the strength to at last admit his failure to pay the rent (if only for one extra week), the voice of the poem admits to everything this poem has been about: his father, even in failure, is "spent, and heroic." His father has never *not* had "powers," power to heal, power to hold a family together, power to "come back sometimes" and enter Albie/Albert through the antigravity pulse of memory, the incontrovertible power of personal myth. Here, the mundane is shown to be more than what we might at first imagine. The mundane *is* mythic. The father in this poem is every bit the hero as "Triphammer. Ghost King. The Scarlet Guardian. Eagleman. Magic Scarab. The Wraith. With their domino masks or their gladiatorial helmets."

The question a poem like "Powers" answers is this: Where do myths come from? They come from those around us. And these myths, having been made into something more, make us recognize the "something more" in the ones upon whom all the spandex and lamé ultimately hang more fittingly. The irony that the poem speaks of is not that superheroes have lame or halting secret identities, but that often it is his or her very secret identity which makes the would-be-hero heroic. The mundane becomes super in having been infused with the "mongoose blood" of itself.

The second function of superheroic myth moves in what at least *appears* to be the opposite direction: making the super mundane. This bathetic move from high mimetic to low is not new to superhero poetry. To back up a bit, the Golden Age of comics starts shortly before Superman and Wonder Woman and Batman's first appearances and continues until, depending on whom one asks, 1956 (when many of the heras and heroes of the past were reimagined by writers and artists whose interests gravitated more toward high mimetic than low) *or* 1961 (with the arrival of the new Marvel pantheon, sprung as if full-grown from the Zeusian brows of Stan Lee and Jack Kirby). The end of the Silver Age and the beginning of what some might call the Bronze (what I call the Platinum) is much more clearly defined.

In 1986, a new breed of writers appeared and with them, an explosion of the most "literary" takes on titles, both old and new, fandom (and now Academe) had yet seen. Suddenly comics seemed to be a garden where "real" literature could take flight—albeit filled with dark knights, swamp things, sandmen, mice, jokers, assassins, and watchmen—and this new paradise meant never having to be ashamed again. Even the academics, even the media, took notice, and fig leaves fell like rain. The classic graphic novels and comics which heralded the birth of the Platinum Age included *The Dark Knight Returns* (1986), *Watchmen* (1986), *Maus* (1986), *Elektra: Assassin* (1986), *Arkham Asylum* (1989), *The Sandman* (1987-1996), others.

Primarily, what these new comics did was to go further than even Marvel did by creating new heroes, rebooting old ones, or, say, allowing a drug plotline to appear in the pages of *Spider-Man*. *The Dark Knight Returns* let us know that Batman could get Alzheimer's and apnea and that Superman's moral superiority could be co-opted by Big Brother. *Maus* showed us that even the Nazi "Uberman" could be defined down into a crude, line-drawn, talking animal. *Watchmen* and *Elektra Assassin* and *Arkham Asylum* all showed the madness lurking beneath the desire to don masks, and *Sandman* let us know that angels, however well-meaning, can make even the lowest levels of hell worse. Each of these paradigm-shifting tales took their grandeur from stripping grandeur away, from de-mythologizing the myth they engaged. But that is only the surface of the myth function.

De-mythologizing can re-mythologize. Hercules seems greater due to his failings. Inanna's sacrifice means more, not less, when we recognize her three days on a "cross," stripped of power, will bring life back to the upper world. Knowing that Batman fears his own psychosis more than the criminals who may share it makes him greater; this knowledge reinvents and reinvigorates the myth that only *seemed* so much larger than the man. Many recent superhero poems take the same tack, two in particular, Lucille Clifton's sequence of Superman poems and Michael Martone's "Sex Lives of the Fantastic Four." These poems let us know that, like the heroes they reincarnate, myths can themselves suffer and rise again, becoming like Obi Wan or Merlin or Mentor, "more powerful than you can possibly imagine." Clifton's sequence reimagines Superman as a "player," perhaps some merely imagined white knight who is, finally, mortal, fallible. The voice says, "... who will come flying after me/ leaping tall buildings/ you?" The poems go on to suggest that it is the speaker, not Superman, who should be seen as the speaker's savior: "lord, man of steel, i understand the cape, the leggings, the whole ball of wax. you can trust me, there is no planet stranger than the one i'm from." In another poem, she asks, "what have you ever traveled toward more than your own safety?"

Ironically, though, these poems do not minimize Superman. Yes, they make him mortal, suggest the speaker should rely on herself more than on some dead world's super son, but ultimately that is the very message of the Christ myth, a matrix of which Superman is part. Christ (and Hopkins) tells us "there is the dearest freshness deep down" flesh. So too, Superman. Clark Kent has always been more "real" than his Kryptonian side. Clifton writes, "sweet jesus, superman, if i had seen you dressed in your blue suit i would have known you." Isn't this how *we* know him? Isn't Clark's buffoonery at the water cooler far more real to us than pushing around planets? But, at the same time, doesn't this fact make the possibility of super acts more super? Can we not imagine ourselves turning back time, to bring Lois back to life, to help our father pay the rent, find a cure for his Alzheimer's, stop the speeding divorce in its tracks? We are all potentially "filthy with kryptonite." Our suits, whether in the closet or in some secret fortress, whether inner or outer, are all blue.

Similarly, Michael Martone's prose poem "Sex Lives of the Fantastic Four" dresses down archetypes, also only to set them flying again. A sequence of four voices, the poem begins with the Invisible Girl ruminating over sex with her husband, Mr. Fantastic. While she considers becoming "translucent," "wiped clear in streaks like a smear of butter melts the white from a paper plate," considers becoming "clarified grease beneath him," Mr. Fantastic ponders folding and refolding himself like a Samurai sword until he is something else entirely, until "elasticity nearing its end, effaced to the point of transparency, my thinning skin becoming, at last, the clear outer covering, at last, of this new creature we create." Both, like the other two voices of the Human Torch and the Thing, ask questions of identity. How can we have someone inside us and still be us? How can we be inside someone and not get swallowed to nothingness? How can we be different, gay, straight, indefinable, and still fit into a society that wants us to protect its rules and values?

Shelley may indeed argue that "in periods of the decay of social life, the drama sympathizes with that decay," and there are those who believe this is precisely what happened in comics in the 80s and in many of today's poems. But it is not so simple. When Sue says, "I see through my lids, through myself, see his cock, clearly, moving inside of the vast and now empty empty space which must be me and must be not me," or when Johnny says, "I can't watch myself all the time. A human touch sets off the human torch. I am captive within my sublime hide," or when Ben says, "I am another other…the public can't begin to see the me that's me," we recognize that the Fantastic Four are not only fantastic, nor are they only four. They are normal, fearful, they are lost, and they are everyone. Being everyone, being fallible, *four*grounds their humanity, but it does what the best myths also do; it complicates what seemed imminently explainable. The paradox: Making the super mundane actually reinvests the mundane with wonder. In this way, both the first and second functions are really the same. We take what *is not* to make what *is*, and what *is* becomes what is not. Either direction takes us toward the sublime, the realm of the mythopoeic.

The last two functions we will visit only briefly. Many superhero poems attempt to revive the superhero, reconnecting the latter half of the name to its ancient origins. Jarrett Keene's "The Human Torch" and Jeannine Hall Gailey's "Wonder Woman Dreams of the Amazon" are but two examples. Part of what happens with myth is that new incarnations are often not recognized as kin to past mythotypes. It is this fact which allows casual readers to attribute to modern myth a lesser status. Other kinds of readers, and many poets, appear to believe otherwise, or at least encourage connections that make us remember the continuum in which superheroes exist. Keene reminds us of several etymologies, words first, then archetype. Of the elements of fire, he writes, "Cesium renders a flame sky blue. Thallium, from the Greek *thallos*, offers a green-shoot. Vanadium of the Isthmus spans a rainbow of colors & is named after the Scandinavian goddess of art & beauty." Words contain history, he tells us, important meanings fossilized by time and use. The same can be said of mythic figures: "In 68 A.D., Nero set fire to Rome to provide inspiration for a new ballad he was composing about the burning of Troy." Though the inferences here are not explicit, Keene groups Johnny Storm with those who would create storm or fire from the past. He connects the very *notion* of storm, of fire, of destruction, with art and beauty. *Sturm und drang* incarnate, Johnny is the hothead Romantic that is also Keene himself. And all are part of a lineage that finds beauty in what burns.

Jeannine Hall Gailey's "Wonder Woman Dreams of the Amazon" lets Wonder Woman herself tell us how the denizens of Paradise Island "named me after their patron Goddess. I was to be a warrior for their kind." Further, Diana says, "I miss my mother, Hippolyta. In my dreams she wraps me tightly again in the American flag..." Here, several "original" antecedents emerge: the Greek myth of Amazons; the idea of a forgotten paradisal island, or Eden; the story of Diana, goddess of the hunt; the tale of Hippolyta, Amazonian queen who fought Hercules; and the American dream itself. All these myth matrices come together in a poem that ends with Wonder Woman saying, "I become everything I was born to be, the dreams of the mother, the threat of the father." *Our* mothers and fathers are Wonder Woman's mothers and fathers. They are our dreams, our myths, our ideals. Sometimes they help us survive or submit, sometimes they make us murder, "mere anarchy loosed upon the world." But, as Yeats would have it, the image out of *Spiritus Mundi* is always there, just at the edge of our thought, awaiting entrance from Paradise into the world of "Men."

Finally, superhero poetry reconnects us to the sublime, to the Romantic, through a "pop" back door. Whether we speak of Greg Santos' "Hulk Smash!," Sherman Alexie's "Totem Sonnets," or Ryan Van Cleave's "The Flash, In Old Age," we must recognize that such poems are a conduit to the divine, to what is, at its very least, an Overstory ever so much larger than us. Perhaps too many of our myths *have* been relegated to the junkyard of history. Perhaps we believe they no longer pertain. We are Postmoderns after all, past the Age of Reason—post-Paine, post-Copernicus, post-Darwin, post-Freud, post-Einstein. But—even in the age Watson and Crick, of Hawking—we can renew our wonder in those old stories, renew our wonder in ourselves and our world, through what myth has already *been* renewed in the retelling. Did we or did we not collectively hold our breath when Superman (Christopher Reeve) said he'd walk again, when he appeared to do just that at the Oscars? Is there or is there not a resurgence, since 9/11, of a need for superheroes? Why else would Spider-Man and Batman be reinventing, rebuilding, renewing New York at the movies? Humans are, as ever, "compelled to serve the power which is seated on the throne of their own soul."

When we encounter superheroes, we hobnob with Homer, we worship Wotan, we confront Krishna. When we write of superheroes, we descend, like Inanna, into the underworld, strip ourselves of what we know, stand naked before our own mortality, our sister, death. When we invite myth into our lives, when we write poetry, when we do the "nothing" Auden speaks of, we do everything. And, as Auden claimed, as Kinnell proposes in "The Bear," those myths enter us even as we enter them, sharing and transfusing that "sticky infusion, that rank flavor of blood, that poetry" by which we live. Like Dickey's sheep child, we go on living in our father's house, we provoke, we raise our kind. In this way, the soul itself is born. We are always already extensions of the Overstory. We are the fetus that feeds on a greater amniotic sac. That fluid moves and grows and pulses, coequal with what it nourishes. Faster than a speeding bullet, wider than the sky. It is what we give birth to. And it gives birth to us. Myth, finally, is parthenogenic. Given enough time, we become the Gods we made. Is it any onder that they look so much like us? Is it any wonder we are drawn to them? They are the marvels we drew. They are the marvels that draw us.

—Bryan D. Dietrich

P. Andrew Miller

ZATANNA'S HAIKU

stenhsif dna egavaelc
eht terces ot cigam seil
ni noitceridsim

Sherman Alexie

FROM *TOTEM SONNETS*

Lenny
Edgar Bearchild
Holden Caulfield
Tess

The Misfit
Sula
Mazie
Tayo

Cacciato
Cecelia Capture
Hamlet
Jim Loney

Daredevil
The Incredible Hulk

Michael Schmeltzer

ORIGIN STORY: ECHOLOCATION

There are monsters
birthed from sonar and shadow,

ones who navigate
through shrieks

and their echoes.
Gunshots. Two dead

in an alley, the bodies
now echoes of the soul.

The surviving child is afraid
because he is alone,

and at night, unlit
by streetlight or moon,

all blood runs black.

~

A child like a shell-casing
once fell into a cave,

and this time he was afraid
because he was not alone.

In his fear he mistook
tumble for tremble, cape for escape.

In that confusion of thought
is where all of us

first convinced the dark
to love us, and everything

we feared (we tell ourselves)
is outside in the light

bright as a muzzle flash.

Christy Porter

WOLVERINE: THE RE-ORIGIN OF SELF

Knowledge is not proof
There are no scars to mark my passage
No marks to indicate
what was done or will be.

Nothing to show
that I was not born
of metal or amalgamation, but of freshening flesh.

I have only this now that
I did not authorize
but must acknowledge:

Adamantium fused to
bone and claws I did not sanction.
With each slice of now
I rend flesh.
Prove bone.
Each claiming a repetition of the original violation.

Re-wounding, it's called in the medical model.
Yet without scars, without proof of change or time
claiming the present sheaths the past
the history, the stories, the memory fragments
the no-proof.

With the fundamental structure of my body altered
to an instrument of rending
no one will remember
my original self
my original talent.

No one will know that
my original gift
was simply to heal.

Andrew Scott Browers

PLEASE DON'T CALL ME CLARK

I.
It's my birthday again, they tell me
and I believe them.
"Make a wish, son," they tell me.

I am always wishing—
wishing on falling stars
and on trains on bridges we pass;
on all powerful things that are beyond
my reach.

I blow them out, my candles.
But not too hard
because cakes are soft
and I don't want Mom
to be mad,

not on the day
they tell me
is my birthday.

II.
Summer is over and the wheat is tall.
I'm tall, too, these days.

Dad and Mom have been talking in low voices late at night
when they think
I can't hear them.

"It can't hurt," Dad says, "Boy's strong as steel."
Mom says nothing, but I hear
the worry in her heart.

So Dad brings me a football
and teaches me
to catch.

He tosses it my way, and it hangs in the air,
wobbling, imperfect,
spiraling wildly against endless blue sky.

When I throw it back,
I make sure it wobbles, too,
as it closes the distance
between fathers and sons.

III.
It's summer again, and I am taller still.
Dad turned out to be right—it didn't hurt.

It got my picture in the papers,
and my name printed in gold
on things in the school's glass case.

But it is not my name.

Men from colleges have started to call us
but Dad tells them all we'll think it over.

Spread in the backseat of her parents' car,
Lana tells me that she's thought it over;
she whispers to me
things I have also thought.

But there are things I dare not try,
punches I'm not sure
that I can pull.

She tells me it's okay, that she understands,
but I know she can't.

I tell myself I will never forget.
I will never forget the taste of her mouth
or the meaning of sacrifice.

IV.
It's springtime, things are budding.

Mom pins a flower on my chest.
Though she knows better, she is careful—
she doesn't like the sight
of blood.

"Be good, son," she says "And open the door for her."

Dad gives me the keys,
he pats my shoulder with a knowing look
I don't understand, but I take the keys
from his aging hand.

V.
Summer comes early, but we're still in school.

In late afternoon heat,
she and I and others sit in the loft of the barn.
We drink Cokes and laugh about the old days,
we talk about the new days, the coming days
And we pretend we are not afraid.

I do not pretend.

I am afraid, and I do not pretend.

There will be time to pretend soon enough
I think as I shine my brand-new glasses
and try not to stare too much
at her shape
in the heat.

Robin Smith

CAPES AND COMICS

Show me a hero and I will write you a tragedy. —F. Scott Fitzgerald

The day your adopted mom left you
at a Shell in exchange for fuel
the cars and hours slipped
into inked twilight and coyotes
yipped around emerald dumpsters

you began to wish not for the warm
back seat of her Volvo,
but the comics you left there:

Superman, Batman, and Spider-Man.
Left by each of their parents
to become something much greater
than a simple hero.

As the last coyote sang to husk
of moon, you tugged the red cape
closer to your shoulders,

felt curb and sidewalk fall away
the world is so much smaller up
where you are born and held
tight by wind.

Haley Lasché

ISSUES OF BREAKING THE MERIDIAN

I was born with wings
as some are born six-fingered,
but wings cannot be amputated—

In high danger
instinct asks the body to unfold away from gravity.

Feathers crave the feel of air,
yet the slight tip of a feather seeking its wind
can tilt a stranger's chin
just enough to ask: *What are you?*

There is no time to listen for wonder,
to prepare for his possible attack. The wing is hidden.

The hiding is the sadness of the other beauty,
the wish borne from denial,
the morning after the dream wound begins to heal.

gerald l. coleman

before it was cool

i was a
nerd before
it was cool

bespectacled
behind a stack
of comics, yeah
i knew that
alcoholic in a
red and gold
alloy-not-iron
suit before
they put his
name in lights
i knew the
blind man
without fear
before they squandered
his devilish
double-d red
reputation in
darkened theaters
with popcorn
littering the floor

back when
clair de lune
was being pumped
into the neighborhood
through grainy
speakers while
star-spangled bomb
pops and orange
push-ups were
being pedaled like
they were crack out

of cold trucks
with faded pictures
of frozen happiness
on the side
i was that
shoe unlaced nerd
with luke cage and
iron fist tucked
under my arm

before
it was cool

i was the
quiet little cutie
grown-ass women
fell in love with
my cheeks were
irresistible to
their bejeweled and
lotioned, long
and manicured
face-pinching fingers
i know now
that what i
saw in their
eyes then, was
either a longing
for saddle-shoed
days gone by
or a desperate wish
for a grown-up
me

stan lee was
my Shakespeare

before
it was cool

while waiting
for my very
own mutant
powers to manifest
themselves
i was taking apart
all my mother's
electronics
screws, boards,
fuses, tubes all
laid out in a row
i was wired
on dismantled
televisions looking
for the secrets
of the universe
all the while raising
her blood pressure
as she walked in on
her brand-new
radio in pieces
giving me that
what-have-i-
brought-into-the-
world look when
i returned it
reassembled, fully
functional

i was a
nerd
before the cool
nonprescription

glasses epidemic
before nostalgia
made chuck taylors
a badge
of honor
back when they
were just cheap
before the ironic
t-shirt renaissance
before they made
batman sane

i was a
nerd
before
it was cool

and that was cool

Gerard Wozek

MY LIFE WITH TAKI MATSUYA

has real meaning. I'm teaching my boy genius
how to read. We pour over ancient alchemical
texts. Memoirs of Madame Blavatsky. A grimoire
penned by King Solomon. When he's not helping
school children to divine their mutant powers, he
shows me how to reshape metal into talismans,
dead car engines into battery packs, glass shards into
water fountains. He's the lonely Wiz Kid, introverted,
shy. He sometimes tells me his secrets. How he crushes
demons with his weaponized Goblin Buster or how
to troubleshoot his supercomputer. At night,
in dreams, Taki imagines he can still dance. I watch
as he balls up the soaked bed sheets over his chest
and cries for the mother and father he lost in a car crash.
I cry with him too. But not even my own emerging
superpowers can help heal the gulf inside him.
When I can no longer quell his violent shaking,
we take off in his flying wheelchair. Holding on
to his shoulders, we etch our way through clouds,
orbit past a flush of dying stars, then onto unknown
galaxies, unnamed worlds.

Gary Jackson

LUKE CAGE TELLS IT LIKE IT IS

Don't believe everything you read.
The exploits you find in my comic
are no more probable
than snow in Sunnyvale.
I'm not as black as you dream.

But a body has to make a living.
And I play the part
better than any. I know
the dangers of believing
every shade of black you see.

In this issue
there's a Mandingo of a man,
dark like olives,
voice as deep as a desert valley
in the dead of night. He smiles
as if he wants to bite your throat,
holds back his teeth
with those bubblegum lips
that he can't help but lick, leaving
the thinnest film of saliva
on the surface.
He's slick
and he's bold
and he's everything you imagine he should be.

Sometimes, you want to be him,
want to see yourself in the silver gleam of his image
and other times you want to be wanted by him.
Crave his brand of desire,
his form of righteousness,
bringing a little black to the world
one *motherfucker* at a time.

No matter how three-dimensional he seems,
know that behind every *jive turkey* uttered
there is not a black mouth, but a white one,
one that dictates who he calls *Nigger*,
to temper the perfect tone of black.

This is the cruelest trick.
Even now, I'm defined by the borders
of my panels, the hue of sienna ink,
an assembly of lines, a rendering of man
splayed across your page.

Chad Parmenter

FROM *BAT & MAN*

So bats conceived you, just as much as Tom?

They stayed, and came again, as many nights
as Tom and Martha did. Like living scarves,
they veiled the windshield while my parents loved.
You'd call that love? I dreamed their wedding white.

"I d-d-do," his stutter, fluttered, spat
at Martha's heart. Her muttered echo stirred
the womb they both assumed was bare, no spark
but nerves.
        But there I germinated, net
of cells and maps of capillary starred
with organs.
        Mother said the wedding march
attracted bats. They charged above the cars
and surged into the crowd, that scattered, lurched,
and scourged them with corsages. Like a scar,
she drew them in. They chased her from the church.

You must have learned of heroes before words.

The nursery I was raised in—arsenal,
where suits of armor rusted to their swords
and soldered armies swarmed before their lord,
myself. I crawled along embroidered snarls
of women woven into carpets dull
from centuries of knees. Their eyeholes bored
into my feet. I felt them. Paintings glared
above—the ancient Waynes, whose perfect scowls
were turning, as they cracked, into the smiles
of skulls.
        At dinner time, a shadow dawned
along my back and drowned the battlefield.
I'd shrink in Mother's shade, her giant hand
a wing I took, that shook, eclipsed and chilled
my own. I loved the Cornish game hens, tan
on silver plates, like torsos on their shields.

Did all your heroes come out of the dark?

We went to Gotham Theater to see
The Mark of Zorro. Tyrone Power wore
the name and cape, eclipsing every score
with gunfire. Such a sweet and distant screen—
I felt the world contract to him and me.
My mother's screams, my father's drunken snore
were shams, or dreams, as blurry as their scars
are now. But then, across the screen, a vein
of darkness ran, like ink, its tip a blade.

Some vandal slashed the screen? Then ran away.
They didn't stop the movie? No, it played,

and Zorro wore a moving wound. Then? Stay
in this, a second. Feel the urge to pray

to him? *He's only light, though.* So is day.

What heroes nursed you in the orphanage?

In Father's leather book of doctor lore—
the bat-masked shaman. Rattles in his wings,
he'd zoom into the spirit world, to bring
the fever-driven patient back to ours.

In Gotham, shaman meant machine—the car,
the cinema, where newsreels lit the flings
of holy criminals who battled gangs,
who went by vigilante. *And they were*

the Shadow? Traveled under every street
with .45s to light his way through hell.

And Phantom? Pantomimed him overseas
on battlefields tiled with Nazi skulls.

And Batman? No. Not him. In violet sheets,
I'd imitate their magic. *Heal by veil?* No. Heal by kill.

A. Van Jordan

THE ATOM

DC Comics, June-July, 1962, Atom #1,
"Master of the Plant World"

It was as if no one had seen me

until I mastered the science

of shrinking my body

down to a particle

level, a basic element

a life so pure

that it was above

all frequencies of critique.

It was as if no one felt

my hand till it was pure vibration,

lighter than a gnat's wing,

on the back of their hand,

not till my touch became

a thought experiment

of memory: people wondering

if they could recall my skin

against theirs and if this recollection

was just that or a new experience—

something impossible yet flesh

and bone. I'm stronger than most men,

but I'm as weak as any man,

too. I fight to save the world

from destruction, but I also fight

to hear my lover, Jean Loring, say Yes

to marriage and to figure out my purpose

in this world. Do you think

if I could have managed my life

at 6' and 180 pounds

I would have shrunk

to near invisibility just to be seen?

Sometimes shrinking to the size

of a coin is a super power;

sometimes it's just a way

to find value in one's life.

Sonya Taaffe

A FIND AT ÞINGVELLIR

You cannot hear the sea-butchering strain of the oars,

the red-bladed ships rowing

from Vinland to the Pillars of Hercules

with the god in the stormwind,

in small iron at their throats,

honor's handclasp and the levin-shock

of a stranger's weight on a spear.

It feels in your hand

not like the molten cooling of meteorites

or the quern-stone of its name,

but a live thing,

excited as St. Elmo's fire

or the quick breath of battle,

copper-wire hilting

singing like a dynamo.

You can hear it humming

thorns and journeys, your inheritance.

Even the gods cannot hold it lightly,

or tightly, or for very long.

Wendy Taylor Carlisle

WONDER WOMAN

Once the comic book opens, your heart
begins its endless search for
wonder embodied in that slick first cover.
Your former life was another art,

required an invisible airplane,
bullet-deflecting bracelets,
the anomaly of a Lone Ranger mask
but the minute you catch on to

...all the strength of Superman plus
all the allure of a good and beautiful woman,
you drop Diana Prince's Golden Lasso,
the doe-eyed gaze and torso tone.

No more need for cartoon and costume.
Bare and apocalyptic,
                    you begin.

Note: Wonder Woman's first cover was *Sensation Comics #1*, January 1942. The italicized lines are from a statement by Wonder Woman's creator, William Moulton Marston.

R. Narvaez

SAVE THE WHITE TIGER

Hector Ayala was a superhero
You probably don't remember
Puerto Rican, from La Isla
Boricua puro puro
He called himself the White Tiger

He attended the same college as Peter Parker,
So, a good role model and all
His powers came from mystical jade amulets
a rainbow of superdudes had abandoned
Hector picked the jewelry out of the trash
If the cops had caught him then
without a receipt...

White Tiger was a master of martial arts
White Tiger wore a head-to-toe white costume
Blanco, todo blanco
His ethnic face, his mustache, his afro,
totally hidden behind a mask of white

His girlfriend's name was Holly

He never got a shot against Galactus
or Thanos or Ultron
He fought street gangs, drug dealers,
someone named the Prowler

White Tiger was an urban superhero
A superhero from the 'hood
Later, they said he developed
an unhealthy addiction to the amulets
An addicted Puerto Rican
Thank you, Marvel Comics

Spider-Man was his friend, Daredevil his lawyer
But in the end Hector Ayala

was convicted of murder
He lost his temper on the stand
That hot Latino temper
Then cops shot him
when he was trying to escape
Not the kind of thing
that ever happens to Batman.
Later on Hector was proven innocent
But by then it was too late
Anyway, it was nice for a little while
to have a Latino superhero
even a white one.

David Stallings

OFF MEDIAL AVENUE

Hair combed into a V
on his forehead, clad in black,
The Avenger slips

from his family's Nashville house
into darkness and power.
With mission to *protect and defend*

he steals along shadow,
peers into Sadie Mack's window. The widow
sits sewing, listening to the radio.

Stream of alert silence, he glides
along a row of trimmed shrubs
to the Todds' side yard. Eyes barely

clearing a family room window sill,
he spies his third-grade friend, Tony
snapping a little sister with red

bath towel. Both are naked.
Their dad yells, "Cut it out!"
The Avenger drops low, scrambles

for home. Safely in bed, hair
brushed back, he lies stunned by this first
taste of the borderlands.

Michael G. Cornelius

FORMATIVE

If I were to speak
the truth—
(and what else is verse for?)
then some credit *must* be
given to the taut camber of
John Wesley Shipp's
flashy Lycra; the
authoritative tone of
super ginger Hal
Jordan as he bossed
around his friends (plus, of
course, that flamboyant
ring); and, *natch*, all,
and I mean *all*,
of Lou Ferrigno's
hulking verdant mass.

Still, to be perfectly
honest
about all this,
it was the crisscross
leather, blonde pageboy,
shaggy underwear and
stentorian bluster of
He-Man that
sooo
made me gay.

R. Narvaez

PETER AND THE SPIDER
After Yeats

A shocking bite: the tiny heart pulsing
Warm atop a graceless boy's sweaty palm
Comes down trembling, skin pierced with a sting,
Mixes his sticky fluids with its own.
How could timid, unschooled hands defy
The swollen body, the clinging hair?
How can a boy, forlorn as a fly,
Elude a touch, even insect, from which flares
Through taut limbs, through weak eyes unwanted scenes:
A towering bridge, a fleshly blonde girl,
And sweet Uncle Ben dead.
                              Standing aglow,
Thus ensnared by the blaze within his jeans,
Did he ingest its nature with its venom
Before the burning fangs could let him go?

P. Andrew Miller

MARVEL WORD PROBLEMS

If Spider-Man can lift 15 tons, can jump over 20 feet, has reflexes 15 times faster than normal, but can't save the people he loves, how do you measure regret?

If Aurora leaves the convent flying at Mach 3 heading east and her brother Northstar leaves Montreal at Mach 5 heading south but stops in New York to come out, what is the speed of acceptance?

If Black Bolt's voice caused the death of his parents and cost his brother his sanity, and he wants to tell Medusa, his wife, he loves her, what is the price of a whisper?

If Apocalypse attacks New York at 5:33 and the X-Men save the day at 8:22 and the mutant protests start at 8:30, what time does the hate stop?

If the Scarlet Witch can control probabilities and marry a synthezoid and have children yet go insane and kill her friends in the Avengers, what are the chances of love in the Age of Ultron?

Ned Balbo

FLASH OF TWO WORLDS

DC Comics, September 1961, The Flash #123, "Flash of Two Worlds":
Jay Garrick, the original Flash, challenges the identity of Barry Allen, the
Silver Age Flash, who has broken the barrier between parallel Earths
through his use of super-speed.

When Gardner Fox, freelance writer
& co-creator of the Flash
(speedy hero in winged boots,
Hermes helmet & a scarlet shirt
lightning bolt emblazoned)
found himself assigned to chronicle
his character's successor,
doubt rose, again, to haunt him:
his archetype changed utterly
to fit the Atomic Age,

Fox found the new Flash lacking:
"police scientist" Barry Allen
was, simply, all too perfect
—crew cut, struck by lightning,
splashed by vials of chemicals
that granted super-speed
through some one-in-a-billion chance,
he raced from page to page.
How could Fox bring back the old Flash—
the original incarnation

who'd vanquished Axis villains
in the throes of WWII,
sudden streak of blue & red
who'd brought Fox his first byline?
The solution was ingenious,
if somewhat bewildering:
from behind his bright red mask
the new Flash declares, straight-faced,
There are actually *two* Earths,

parallel worlds that coexist,
pulsing slightly out of sync
yet somehow sharing time & space,
alternating infinitely,
one bright, the other dark—
which is why, whirling at top speed
for a benefit performance,
faster than eyes can follow
Barry vanishes from sight,
having accidentally torn the shield
that separates both worlds.

Displaced, on a different Earth,
he finds his elder namesake,
catches on, concludes a Higher Power
decreed that they would meet
but already knows this proto-Flash
from reading old *Flash Comics*
to whose writer—yes, you guessed it,
Gardner Fox—strange dreams appeared, mind
attuned to off-world exploits, driven
to type up all he'd seen, quantum

mechanics fused with deep sleep
to inspire bi-monthly tales.
In settling old debts, Fox placed
the scribe inside the myth, showed
those hacks who owned the trademark:
Gardner Fox gave them the Flash.
Tireless through the years, he'd write
spy novels, sci-fi, Westerns, porn
under a score of pen names but
would forfeit his true calling
by asking for a raise, Blue Cross

from editors who'd figured out
he, too, could be replaced.
                    In a world
unseen, somewhere, he still lives,
typing out new scripts, well paid,
his imagination's maze struck by
new flashes of inspiration, pages
piling up so fast that he, too,
sometimes loses track, secure
beyond the gateway to some other world.

Note: In reworking the history of DC's comic book character and the life of Gardner Fox, "Flash of Two Worlds" overlooks the contributions of editor Julius Schwartz and artist Carmine Infantino to the revival of the Flash, and of artist Harry Lampert to co-creating the original character. Sources include Gerard Jones and Will Jacob's *The Comic Book Heroes: The First History of Modern Comic Books from the Silver Age to the Present* (Prima: Rocklin, CA: 1997).

Travis Kurowski

SPACE OPERA (V)

Lines taken from the comics and words of Jack Kirby (1917-94)

But here in this oxygen atmosphere the enemy has broken through our
para-demon air defense; their atomic structure is shifting, compacting.
This is not the New York I saw in the micro-film library. This well could be
the prelude to the most dangerous adventure of our career. This hideout is
rigged and booby trapped to kill in a thousand ways.

One night, the evil genius went too far. He has vanquished the Mechano-
Monster. He's forgotten himself—he's attacking like a barroom brawler.
With a hostile race in a nightmare world.

Make way for some real action, boys. Iron bars do not a prison make.
My anatomy was self-taught. Do I walk amidst the civilized world as a
mythical god? I've got a world to conquer. Perhaps by using this as a lever,
I can move the boulder? Come see what weirdies I've dreamed up for you.

    And other terrible devices are sprung into motion;

        And something inside rushes out into the calamitous night.

Christine Stewart-Nuñez

EACH NIGHT, HIS OTHER LIFE

Into his 'toon body—penciled
biceps bulging, jeans filled
with thick-as-tree-trunk thighs—
her husband morphs at midnight.

Issues of *The Punisher*
and classic *Spider-Man* litter
the hardwood floors, relieved
of their protective sleeves.

Wham! Pow! When balloons
of dialogue float on their bedroom
walls, he prepares to leave,
tiptoes past his son who dreams

of little llamas, grouchy lady-
bugs, Chihuahuas, candy
canes. She composes the bed's
blank page. Dagger-edged,

sleek, he walks Main: his shadow
startles a drunk—keys fall down,
lost at the car's door; a light
lit foils a man casing a silent

house. Sunrise. He slips into bed:
cheek scarred, shirt smeared,
foot creased. Who needs a double
life? Gloss leaves his lips supple,

muffling his story. She's tired
and her version's inked in red,
so she caresses his clothed
arm, pulls sheets over them both.

Alex Ruiz

LIVING IN GOTHAM

My heart is Darker than the Knight because
      I don't need Batman to start Robin the city. I been
Injected with Poison Ivy. The need to steal is strong,
      Even if it is a Pennyworth. My neighborhood is scary
Like a Scarecrow, filled with Two-Faced Jokers who
      Riddle a bunch of bullshit, trying to Warner Brother.
I'm not trying to hear anything from a dude who
      Is in and out of the Asylum. I have no time. I'm
Trying to get me a Catwoman from DC and when
      I'm done with her, she'll be walking like a Penguin.
Then it is back to the Robin so I can get rich like
      Bruce Wayne. Buy a Batmobile and some jewelry,
My nickname can be Mr. Freeze. Buy a big mansion
      On the Adam West side. Have my own Batcave
With a personal gym so I can be bigger than Bane.
      And nothing can be better sharing the wealth with
My Justice League and my Julie Madison.

Wesley McNair

THE THUGS OF OLD COMICS

At first the job is a cinch, like they said.
They manage to get the bank teller a couple of times
in the head and blow the vault door so high
it never comes down. Money bags line the shelves
inside like groceries. They are rich, richer
than they can believe. Above his purple suit the boss
is grinning half outside of his face.
Two goons are taking the dough in their arms
like their first women. For a minute nobody sees
the little thug with the beanie is sweating drops
the size of hot dogs and pointing
straight up. There is a blue man flying
down through the skylight and landing with his arms
crossed. They exhale their astonishment
into small balloons. "What the..." they say,
"What the..." watching their bullets drop
off his chest over and over. Soon he begins to talk
about the fight against evil, beating them half to death
with his fists. Soon they are picking themselves up
from the floor of the prison. Out the window
Superman is just clearing a tall building
and couldn't care less when they shout
his name through the bars. "We're trapped!
We got no chance!" they say, tightening their teeth,

thinking, like you, how it always gets down
to the same old shit: no fun, no dough,
no power to rise out of their bodies.

John Ashbery

FARM IMPLEMENTS AND RUTABAGAS IN A LANDSCAPE

The first of the undecoded messages read: "Popeye sits in thunder,
Unthought of. From that shoebox of an apartment,
From livid curtain's hue, a tangram emerges: a country."
Meanwhile the Sea Hag was relaxing on a green couch: "How pleasant
To spend one's vacation *en la casa de Popeye*," she scratched
Her cleft chin's solitary hair. She remembered spinach

And was going to ask Wimpy if he had bought any spinach.
"M'Love," he intercepted, "the plains are decked out in thunder
Today, and it shall be as you wish." He scratched
The part of his head under his hat. The apartment
Seemed to grow smaller. "But what if no pleasant
Inspiration plunge us now to the stars? *For this is my country.*"

Suddenly they remembered how it was cheaper in the country.
Wimpy was thoughtfully cutting open a number 2 can of spinach
When the door opened and Swee'pea crept in. "How pleasant!"
But Swee'pea looked morose. A note was pinned to his bib. "Thunder
And tears are unavailing," it read. "Henceforth shall Popeye's
        apartment
Be but remembered space, toxic or salubrious, whole or scratched."

Olive came hurtling through the window: its geraniums scratched
Her long thigh. "I have news!" she gasped. "Popeye, forced as you
        know to flee the country
One musty gusty evening, by the schemes of his wizened, duplicate
        father, jealous of the apartment
And all that it contains, myself and spinach
In particular, heaves bolts of loving thunder
At his own astonished becoming, rupturing the pleasant

Arpeggio of our years. No more shall pleasant
Rays of the sun refresh your sense of growing old, nor the scratched
Tree-trunks and messy foliage, only immaculate darkness and
        thunder."
She grabbed Swee'pea. "I'm taking the brat to the country."

"But you can't do that—he hasn't even finished his spinach,"
Urged the Sea Hag, looking fearfully around at the apartment.

But Olive was already out of earshot. Now the apartment
Succumbed to a strange new hush. "Actually it's quite pleasant
Here," thought the Sea Hag. "If this is all we need fear from spinach
Then I don't mind so much. Perhaps we could invite Alice the Goon
        over—" she scratched
One dug pensively—"but Wimpy is such a country
Bumpkin, always burping like that." Minute at first, the thunder

Soon filled the apartment. It was domestic thunder,
The color of spinach. Popeye chuckled and scratched
His balls: it sure was pleasant to spend a day in the country.

Matthew Hittinger

ORANGE COLORED SKY

And not just because it's my favorite
        color, but when Diana Prince spins, her

nimbus fills me with glee and glow and when

I was a boy I wore my mother's high
        heels and wrapped my Binky around my neck

like a cape and then coiled it at my side

my blanket of truth and I spun and spun
        arms outstretched and wanted that light to fill

me, envelop me the way I saw it

change Lynda Carter on TV and one
        time she was the guest on the Muppet Show

and I clicked around the basement Rec room

kicking open the doors to "the other
        side" as we called it—where my father's work

bench and the furnace, where my brother set

up his D&D figurine painting
        table, where each Christmas we'd raise the train

platform, and where forgotten furniture

loomed in half-shadows—through here I kicked—Flash—
        kick—Bam—*kick*—Alakazam—*double kick*—

for in heels I could deflect the shadows

like bullets, my wrists wondrous, and when I
        returned from "the other side" to the Rec

room's wood panels and lamp shades, this leaning

toward became learning toward, and I would sit
        visible to all as I piloted

an invisible jet through the orange sky.

Denise Duhamel & Maureen Seaton

POPEYE'S PEP-UP EMPORIUM

Olive eats the spinach to save herself
when Popeye's working out with Brutus—
there he is hanging out with his rival while
she dangles perilously in roller-skates
over a shark-filled pool. The *Godzilla* theme
swells as Popeye does his hundredth biceps curl,
oblivious as a sleeping lizard,
pumped as papier-mâché. Olive, meanwhile,
retrieves a can of spinach from her purse.
Her nail file doubles as an opener
and she pries off the lid with her pearly teeth,
gulps it down and flips to safety like a gymnast.

Chad Parmenter

BATELLITE, BATELLITE OF LOVE

for (and after) Marc McKee

And you think to yourself what a
wonderful underworld, but Batman's
been turning it into one for so long,
dispensing justice, dependable as Pez,
and no melt of the moment frozen in him,
where his parents die in a storm
he plays eye to, his mask black
and blue, his courage like sugar
transfigured by caramelizing crimes.
So is his grimace like happiness
shrinkwrapped in syntax, does the volt
of his pulse shock him hot? No, go
with him out of the alleyways'
shadow mazes, into the moonlight
that inks us mask-blank, look
how it violet-plates the Gotham Bay
waves, wait for the bats to flutter
up carrying narrative accelerant—
a batoscope to hold to sky. At his white
eye, it says what he'd fear, if
he could: aliens have graffitied
the Batellite again. From here,
he sees its riveted wings, its teeth
antennae now spraypainted halo-
gold, but can't make it out. "Up yours,
earthlings," or some patly gangsta
alien slang will take a freaking day
in inky space with the batsandblaster,
and the fanboys, theoptic eyes
shining on this comic book,
pray for it to be a trap, and not
to be a trap, pray his blue hands
to fail at the rocket fighter's
ignition, a holdover from the camp
1960s, its red echo of art deco
rusted toward blood, pray
as he kicks its engine, say thanks
when it sputters. Starts. Lifts off.

Batman sublimates this planet like
a hidden meaning. The Batellite
calls him, and he lands on its wing,
to feather-dust the droppings of
space mice from their crenellations,
and here, for some dream of a reason,
he can breathe. He can pull in
the coal, six-billion year night, sigh
out all of his stresses, kick back
without kicking off into the radii
of asteroids. The graffiti—by the girl
my mind won't quit inking bride-white;
it says I do, but I don't know that yet,
and he breathes it in, perfume of a
plotline atomized, or is it the first
fume of morning dew in your nose,
its crystal trickle not like a penciling
of the Joker's acid-blasting flower, no
it's like light on that one field, that
one morning, where you outran
your fear of running fast, that light
on that kind of new-born green
let you forget you were made of lead,
but, batshit, the whole craft is moving
now. Batman motored the batellite
out of its orbit, as love distracted me.
He's radioed the coast guard SKK
I'M CRASHLANDING IN THE
BAY. Dolly in like Google Earth,
you'll see Commissioner Gordon
orbiting in cigar-hearted mist. Cities
are grids. This one is, too. PHOOM
is the sound of him phooming home,
HMM is the sound of the cosmic
optimism he brings with him. Will
the city survive this epiphany? Will
we? Tell me. I'm waiting to write it.

Christine Stewart-Nuñez
WONDER WOMAN RELAXES

Closing her steno pad at five, Diana
contemplates cuisine, not the break
room's lime JELL-O. Superfood:

spinach sautéed in olive oil, quinoa-
pilaf with Turkish apricots. Once
home, glasses off, hair ponytailed,

sweatpants on, she slices a pineapple
like it's cream cheese. As she juliennes
jalapeños, she needs no magic bracelet;

golden lassos won't quicken the task.
She admires the cut's discernment.
When her man's in trouble, Wonder

Woman busts him out; slaps, slugs,
strikes, what does it matter if she
breaks a nail or three? Her man

doesn't see her. Post-mission, he's
safe watching TV, and Diana's free
to pummel villains with Superman,

Aquaman. They love her feminine
touch. Tonight, comics will wait.
Skimming across the dusty wine

rack, she chooses a cab, Opus One,
'85, and pulls out the company,
crème brûlée. On the balcony, she

dines, the city's honks and calls,
her symphony. Sirens pulse
through her veins like a heartbeat.

Shayla Lawson

EPISTOLARY OF THE X: STORM

If you are the unstoppable force, I am
the insatiable wound. I was Grace

Jones before Grace Jones knew grace.
My hair Mohican, mercurial eagle feathers

blazing. I was Petra cool ascending from the rock
and the cape wore me. We flapped like an edge

and the elements cursed: *Ororo Munroe Ororo Munroe*
midnight in every abominable scorch of sunset.

I magnetize the Earth. Its faint perfume rescinds
into autumn—winter—electricity could not hold it.

I have been everything we needed a woman for; at times
my hair slung it full weight to the sea's electronic bottom

[Electric Boogaloo]. I earned the wind to call its words.
I taught the thieves to thief. I resurrect as one

in doubled mirrors fractals many :: And when you
had Halle Berry play us in a botched wig we were not pleased ::

Let us speak as blustered gale. Let you fashion the face less
conviction; I cyclone the notorious in furious funnel.

Let thou make minstrels out of that. I do not always believe
they knew I was Black but they knew I was right— as rain,

as some thunderous consequential, concertos of dust
gesticulating, a dorsal moon of crescent bed to gnash

—You think of me as spell but I am always coming—
Blue as the eye and blue as the iris, blue as Gulf Stream

retracted, blue as flint spark, blue as the ember underbelly
to clouds, blue as trouble to the logos: *aurora borealis.*

Blue to the halted heist, blue to any man
draining every kind of light, blue as blew

in the face. Blue as the doll, held by girl, looking
just like me. Blue if I wasn't lightning enough.

Jeannine Hall Gailey

WONDER WOMAN DREAMS OF THE AMAZON

I miss the tropes of Paradise—green vines
roped around wrists, jasmine coronets,
the improbable misty clothing of my tribe.

I dream of the land of my birth. They named
me after their patron Goddess.
I was to be a warrior for their kind.

I miss my mother, Hippolyta.
In my dreams she wraps me tightly
again in the American flag,

warning me, "Cling to your bracelets,
your magic lasso. Don't be a fool for men."
She's always lecturing me, telling me

not to leave her. Sometimes she changes
into a doe, and I see my father
shooting her, her blood. Sometimes,

in these dreams, it is me who shoots her.
My daily transformation
from prim kitten-bowed suit to bustier

with red-white-and-blue stars
is less complicated. The invisible jet
makes for clean escapes.

The animals are my spies and allies;
inexplicably, snow-feathered doves
appear in my hands. I capture Nazis

and Martians with boomerang grace.
When I turn and turn, the music plays louder,
the glow around me burns white-hot,

I become everything I was born to be,
the dreams of the mother,
the threat of the father.

Greg Santos

Gotham Knight

I am the fog that chokes the air.
The bat that's tangled in your hair.

I hide beneath your bed at night.
I am The Rife, criminals, The Rife.

I am Vengeance. I am Wrath.
I roam the subway with the rats.

I am The Night that you don't see.
Superman's got nothing on me.

Spider-Man spins a dainty web.
I make bad guys really dead.

Green Lantern's ring makes a pretty light.
I don't do pretty. I do fight.

I taught Charlie Sheen to win.
I chucked Chuck Norris in a bin.

Stallone, Willis, & Van Damme:
All nobodies. I'm the man.

Mike Tyson?
Baddest man on the planet.

I'm like the Death Star.
I blow up planets.

Rhyme planet with planets?
I break the rules.

I am The Batman.
I do what I—KAPOW!

Denise Duhamel & Maureen Seaton

XENA: WARRIOR PRINCESS

I run through the muck of New Zealand
side-kicking fiends. Sword-fighting demons
add to the quackery of my even-
tempered sidekick's medical practice.
I'm good with a sword and herbal poultices
to cure my own wounds. Don't mistake my bruises
for mistakes. Every one was destined to boost
TV ratings and jolt the audience
from microwave popcorn and frozen fish sticks.
You can be me for Halloween. In fact,
I come in all cultures now, scratch
my surface, I'm complete as Barbra Streisand.
She can keep her press-on nails, her dopey fans.
I have warrior work to do, silvery plans.

Stephen D. Rogers

CAP'N

My name is Steve Rogers

Steve Rogers is Captain America

"Captain America" is how I'm hailed

From across the quad

Through stacks of warehouse pallets

As I join my friends at play

The Captain has no superpowers

No superpowers have I

We're alike in so many ways

Except he died

And then he didn't

But I never stopped fighting the Nazis

In my own way

Katharyn Howd Machan

No, Superman Was Not The Only One

In secret, Lois Lane wore coins and jewels
draped perfectly against the naked skin
she perfumed with wild jasmine, taunting fools
who'd denigrate her dance as snaky sin.
She called for drumbeat, shook the stage apart
with shift and shimmy, crescent arms upraised
to show the world the power of her art
and how on Earth the Goddess should be praised.
In silvered silk, her pinned-up hair set free,
she swayed and spun and seemed almost to fly
above the smoky air, almost to be
a bird, a plane, sublime in midnight sky.
No morning news reported what she did;
even from Clark she kept her cymbals hid.

Jeannine Hall Gailey

FEMALE COMIC BOOK SUPERHEROES

are always fighting evil in a thong,
pulsing techno soundtrack in the background
as their tiny ankles thwack

against the bulk of male thugs.
With names like Buffy, Elektra, or Storm
they excel in code decryption, Egyptology, and pyrotechnics.

They pout when tortured, but always escape just in time,
still impeccable in lip gloss and pointy-toed boots,
to rescue male partners, love interests, or fathers.

Impossible chests burst out of tight leather jackets,
from which they extract the hidden scroll or antidote,
tousled hair covering one eye.

They return to their day jobs as forensic pathologists,
wearing their hair up, donning dainty glasses.
Of all the goddesses, these pneumatic heroines most

resemble Artemis, with her miniskirts and crossbow,
or Freya, with her giant gray cats.
Each has seen this apocalypse before.

See her perfect three-point landing on top of the chariot,
riding the silver moon into the horizon,
city crumbling around her heels.

CB Droege

RING (SOLDIER)

He is strong.   I am stronger.
I found him:
Man of   courage.
Man   of   willpower.
Still   just   a   man;   a   weapon.
He thinks he carries me into battle,
but he is wrapped around my finger.
He is the bright green emblem
which I carry as a standard.
I   am   the   soldier.
I am the hero.
He is strong.   I am stronger.

Amanda Chiado

CATWOMAN RISES

They leave me for dead.
A cosmic storm of men
like rain tunnels
of galactic dust.
When you are heavy,

body heavy, under six feet
of mud, it grinds
you into another winter.
You become the living
dead. The dead you, writhing.

The live you, invisible.
Every night in alley ways,
inspired by a siren's song,
I wait for the man who thinks
his hands are formidable gods,

a hungry-tongued wannabe
with a hot house for a heart.
I am always there when they come.
They smile when I say,
the day I died, I started to live.

Tara Betts

OYA INVITES STORM TO TEA

If you are going to play me,
why don't you wear purple?
Blue eyes and washed out white
mane twisted about your head.

Seems like you had a tumble
due to a flutter of my hands.
Drafts and tombstone seats
are not always comfortable
or inviting, but some people
feel the same way about me,
which is why I invited you,
distant daughter. Comic
book pretenses fail to do
your powers justice.

Summoning typhoons
and hailing rainstorms
are a flash of talents.
Dear girl, you can
change climates,
battle smoke
that hazes the sky,
sweep away toxins
seeping into the earth.

The dead whisper daily
prophecies, nudge me
to yank you
from Stan Lee's grip
to discover horizons
shifted simply
by raising your arms.

You can stop hurricanes,
start them, level houses,

raise water, ignite
anything in the open
urging of your palms.

You are change, clean as
seasons and destruction.
The world will always need you.
Your eyes are not vacant.

I hope you like your tea hot
with steam and ginger root.
Sip deeply. You will need
all the strength that comics

cannot imagine.

Jarret Keene

THE HUMAN TORCH

Man acquires a soul, but remains only a body.
       —Norman O. Brown, *Life Against Death*

Could burst into flame
at will. Despite
the name, he was
originally an android
created by a
mad professor.
Nemesis: The Sub-
mariner. Fire vs.
Water. Later, a teenage
hothead with an
affinity for fast
cars. Comics
Code prohibited
burning people,
throwing fireballs.
Johnny Storm?
Just what kind
of name is
that? Sounds
funny today,
but maybe
in the 60s
it was cool &
there was plenty
oxygen to burn:
Flame on!

Compounds of
rubidium, when
burned in a flame,
give off a ruddy
glow. Cesium
renders a flame
sky blue. Thallium,
from the Greek
thallos, offers
a green-shoot.
Vanadium of the
Isthmus spans
a rainbow of
colors & is
named after the
Scandinavian goddess
of art & beauty. In 68 A.D.,
Nero set fire to
Rome to provide
inspiration for
a new ballad
he was composing
about the burning
of Troy. He blamed
the Christians, since
they were scapegoats.

Jon Tribble

WIND TUNNEL

When you are The Atom—not just a building
block in someone else's idea of what strange
magnet attracts and pins the iron filings on top
to the top, in-between and bottom to the bottom
and in-between—a superhero when you get up
in the morning, a superhero when you lie down
in a king-size matchbox bed at night, when a spin
around your block has all the quaint charm
that comes with hills of dust and lint the size
of Texas, when every smell and all the flavors

have a zip code, a sticky calling card that flavors
the fingertips of your red gloves, when building
relationships never worked since you know *size
matters* and there are all the circus-act-strange
positions you can't begin to describe, no charm
or talisman ever enough to convince who's on top
you're even in the room, no post office or spin-
the-bottle worth it when you're the last boy, bottom
monkey pulled from the barrel, and if it were down
to you and the Barry White behemoth getting up

and blocking the sun with his belly, she will turn up
on his arm, not yours, since she can taste the flavors
of his lips while you're lucky to get jotted down
—even noticed—and while you are off building
something new to save the world, the real bottom-
line in this equation has been totaled, and the size
absent from your weighty shortcomings won't spin
into anything other than the fact that you are a strange
little freakshow all your own in this carnival big top
and the flea circus is the only place you'll charm

the boys and girls, ladies and gentleman, the charm
and grace of a leaf on the breeze as the fan turns up
the force in the magnifying chamber where like a top

you twirl in your blue secret identity, while the flavors
of cotton candy and popcorn drip from the strange
mouths gaping at your act, confetti spilling down
to join you in the aerodynamic ride, another spin
uncorking a shining maelstrom of pressure building
from the fan blades pushing around twice-your-size
coins of gold paper to gild the cage from bottom

to top while you work without a net, the bottom
well of gravity now releasing you from its charm
and call, your trapeze a wire act rewarding the size
you do not have, mass that has never shown up
when you stepped on a scale, less and less building
toward an impressive zero (though you won't top
out at nothing even if you wish you could spin
the wheel back into *negative* numbers), the flavors
will disappear in the rush around you, a world down
to the elemental—forces you no longer think strange:

trust that air in its strange shapes and imposing size
will receive you from the bottom of your soles and spin
a web softer than down to hold you high, lift you up
like kissing a horseshoe, a charm to open the very top
of the sky, its flavors sustaining, a deep core building.

Hilda Raz

WONDER WOMAN'S RULES OF THE ROAD

WONDER WOMAN'S RULES OF THE ROAD

1. The wall? Walk around. Your legs work, don't they?

2. Wear armor at vulnerable sites. Perfume at pulse points?
   Better, silver bracelets.

3. Learn from heros: tools extend range.

4. The best asset is a wise mother, better a goddess.

5. Absent a mom, girlfriends, comrades.

6. Bind loose hair with a fillet. Keep your face exposed.

7. Anger is power.
   Justice is power.
   Make laws when laws don't suffice (*Herland*)

8. Stand with legs apart: a triangle is more stable than a stick.

9. Avoid camouflage.

10. Don't tangle your legs in a cape.

11. Strong abs are to die for.

WONDER WOMAN'S BRACELETS

Do they cover scars, a suicide attempt? Self-mutilation? Cigarette burns, tiny cuts, gauze and band-aids? In the 60s, you bet. Those mad girls who wrote. Controlled hysteria. Let loose. Therapy. My jewelry box, top left drawer. A trio of silver cuffs (one a spare). The water serpent belongs now to him. (Him?) You.

In the 50s, they were armor. Underneath, perfume at pulses, why? The flutter to waft scent to the boys. I lift my wrist in chemistry class, breathe in. The naked wrist.

Clamp-on bracelets so veins, those incipient geysers, hide. The closed and vulnerable wrists flash like shoulder points under iodine-oil at the beach. In sand, sun, and waves, all flash and movement. Never take them off. What's underneath's taboo.

WONDER WOMAN AND THE DISRUPTED BODY

Imagine Wonder Woman with one breast. Draw her costume.
Alter the top. Only one bracelet. Is it wider? The wooden boot.

WONDER WOMAN'S RULES OF THE ROAD – 1962

1. Watch your wrists. Cut, they're geysers: sexual, lethal. Decorate all death sites, pleasure points: earlobes, throat, labia, lips, elbows, wris...t(s) with scent.

2. Your inner arms, thin and veiny. Perfume daubs won't save you. Silver bands, wide at both wrists, may. They deflect your own gestures, others.

3. Flaunt your belly if it's flat, muscled. Abs are to die for.

4. Stretches every day; don't forget the shoulders. Bounce light from the chin, collarbone, especially in motion. Be in motion. Bounce_____from the wrists.

5. Those headaches? Nothing but a slipped halo, a fillet binding your forehead, a princess crown.

6. Brunettes have more choices.

7. Learn the uses of tools: a whip, a lightning bolt: watch and learn.

8. Flaunt your legs. They work, don't they?

9. Boots, always.

10. Tampons don't show at the beach.

11. Your legs work, don't they?

WONDER WOMAN'S COSTUME AND ADDRESS

How come she gets to wear her swimsuit in the city? How come her boots don't wrinkle? How come her top and bottom don't match? How come she gets to wear earrings with her leotard? How come she doesn't have to wear glasses? How come red, white, and blue isn't tasteless? How come she doesn't have to wear stockings? How come her lipstick's Fire & Ice? How come she lives with girls on an island? Is there an island of girls? Show some respect!

WONDER WOMAN AND DAUGHTERS

She didn't have one, but she could've.

Ryan Bradley

HAIKUS FROM SUPERVILLAINS TO THE PEOPLE THEY LOVE

GREEN GOBLIN TO GREEN GOBLIN II
Tried to be involved.
Helicopter parenting.
Forgive me, Harry.

JOKER TO BATMAN
Bruce, Bruce, Bruce. Why kids?
It's criminal negligence,
not me that kills them.

MAGNETO TO PROFESSOR X
Sorry for your legs,
but I only broke them once.
Do be more careful.

DARKSEID TO HIMSELF
Killed Batman. No point.
I shoot death rays out my eyes
but no one stays dead.

MYSTIQUE TO PROFESSOR X
Do you need maybe,
a permission slip for
Nightcrawler and Rogue?

SABRETOOTH TO WOLVERINE
Your books sell better
without romantic interests,
so I kill them, Bub.

John Rodriguez

DEATHWISH

People ask me what could possibly make anyone want
to live in Gotham City, a panel away from death,
as if I have a fetish for one of these psychopaths
who walks the streets with a scythe, or razor-sharp umbrella:
Don't you know you may end up facedown on a cover page,
some artist's initials written in the pool of your blood?
I grin at them—those hopeless bystanders of safe pages,
the hotdog vendor who gives extra mustard to the mild-
mannered, the un-clever girlfriend who gets abandoned once
the train blindly lunges forward into oblivion,

the bomb tick-tick-ticking underneath the tracks up ahead—
because we Gothamites know tragedy, yes. Who feels safe
anywhere in this comic universe? There's a crisis
somewhere, a psychic gorilla with a plan to conquer
our species. How about you? What keeps you safe? A jet plane?
Where is it? Is it invisible? When all hope is gone
will you dive underwater to live among the merfolk,
and talk to dolphins with your mind? No speedster rescues us,
arriving like a prayer to shift us from the bullet.
No intergalactic peacekeeper bubbles us safely

in a green force field. I do not live here for the murder,
but for the vengeance. Certainly, Gotham City has more
killers per capita than their cities, more killers than
one writer can imagine, but what do you think about
some bulletproof alien god lecturing a kingpin
(two faces, two guns) to change his ways? Be impervious,
no one cares, but be a man—bone, blood and will—who can die,
who can suffer like you, but refuses to, why even
the guilty pause. I stay here for him. I know if I do
die, slit open in one our myriad alleyways,

the searchlight will part skyscrapers and sear clouds. The Batman,
his day spent forging boomerangs, forever boomerangs,
will begin his obsessive manhunt. My killer will soon

be disarmed and bludgeoned by fist and heel, assaulted with
learned, rhythmic pounding, his teeth will be knocked out, he will be
hung upside-down from a streetlight, soaked in his own urine
and blood, waiting for the fat, heavy-handed detective
to blow smoke in his face and drag him to Blackgate Prison.
I'm promised this in Gotham, where I am a bit player,
a nameless citizen destined to be murdered before

the splash page, perhaps I'll answer a doorbell and be shocked,
literally, by a joy-buzzer handshake with the wrong
clown, his white, smiling face of death the last image I see.
I may be shot, frozen solid, or eaten by a man
who thinks himself a crocodile. Here in Gotham City
I stay for justice. I know something may happen to me,
cruel and terrible, as fatal and unfair as a whim
a writer more intuits than reasons, more feels than thinks.
In my throes, should I be given a speech bubble, I'll say,
Please...for all my loyalty...let there be a reckoning.

Jeannine Hall Gailey

JOB REQUIREMENTS: A SUPERVILLAIN'S ADVICE

Grow up near a secret nuclear testing site.
Think Hanford, Washington. Oak Ridge,
Tennessee. North and South Dakota
are riddled with them. Your father—is he
an eccentric scientist of some sort? Did you
show early signs of a "supergenius" IQ?
Experience isolation from "normal" childhood
activities? (Multiple traumatic incidents welcome.)
Physical limitations, such as an unusual but poetic disease
or deformity due to mutation, are preferred;
problems due to accidents involving powerful
new weaponry or interactions with superheroes
are also acceptable. (Develop flamboyant
criminal signatures. Adopt antisocial poses.)
A lack of respect for authority figures such as
world governments is a must.
Fashionable knack for skin-tight costumes
(masks, hooks, extra-long nails) considered a plus.
Study jujitsu or krav maga.
Practice creative problem solving;
for example, that lipstick could be poisoned,
that spiked heel a stabbing implement.
Remember, you are on the side
of the laws of thermodynamics. Entropy
is a measure of disorder.
Chaos, destruction, death: these are your instruments.
Use them wisely. You are no mere mortal.
Don't lose your cool if captured; chances are,
you can already control minds, bend metal to your whim,
produce, in your palms, fire.
In the end, you are the reason we see the picture;
we mistrust the tedium of a string of sunny days.
We like to watch things crumble.

Jason Mott

A DREAM REMEMBERED TWO DAYS AFTER MY FATHER ENTERED HOSPICE

Captain Marvel got nuked; the sky cried lightning;
Batman was shot—failing at heroing—just like his father;
Wonder Woman threaded her sword through the big Slavic's
spine—I forget his name; The Flash shimmered in a pool of red—
both ankles shattered, at last the eyes of man could catch him;
Captain America lost his shield and his arm—just stood there
holding the bloody stump with a gleam of joy flooding his eyes;
and the bombs kept falling, and thunder ate the world
and, somewhere, Lex Luthor watched the whole thing on CNN
while IVs drilled into his collapsing veins, his food came siphoned
through rubber tubes, cancer webbed in his lungs and marbled
in his prostate, cirrhosis drank his liver, diabetes ate his ability to feel
his legs—the doctors kept screaming "amputation"—
the medical bills bankrupted him; and out in black-skied Kansas
the wheat fields smoldered, Clark Kent folded in on himself—
mild manners gave him nothing but papier-mâché fallout shelters
full of regret; SUPERMAN fell on both knees, his hands caked
in embers and heavy, wet Kryptonian tears, and all he could hear—
somewhere, somewhere very close, somewhere, somewhere far away—
was a black-haired orphan, swaddled in red, screaming, screaming, screaming;
and Captain Marvel was less than a remnant; and the sky sobbed fire,
and the Earth gave up mothering; Batman gave in to anemia—
permeable flesh, porcelain bones—and Gotham ran red;
Wonder Woman cut out her ovaries—finally, after all those years
of holding on, finally; The Flash tried running on his hands, stumbled, fell,
thudded to the ground; and the bombs were still falling,
and ash owned the sun, and Lex Luthor still wouldn't die—
of cancer or diabetes or high blood pressure or contentment—
he watched from his bed, green in his eyes; and—even with Clark Kent limp
and wilted—there was more MAN than Super, his cape sackcloth from soot,
he couldn't get up off his knees—he couldn't stop his cracked hands
from trembling—out in the middle of that smoldering, Kansas wheat field;
a figure lingered there, in the staccato of Ragnarok, dancing a nervous jig,
a bright-eyed voodoo priest, a dark, young boy—aged seven—faltering,
and when he spoke, he said: "His cancer will come for you too one day,

just like this."

Barbara Hamby

NIETZSCHE EXPLAINS THE ÜBERMENSCH TO LOIS LANE

No, no, no, no—he doesn't even have nerves of steel. No
point asking him to save you, ma'am, he's more likely to rescue
rain from the street. Born on your block, not Krypton, he's
terror with a capital "T," the beautiful mind you
vain dames can't see for the mascara on your lashes. You saw
exactly nothing when you clapped eyes on him, a nerdy
zip, not even head of the class, just skulking in the back, a
brilliant light in a room full of blind men. But when he rises, havoc
descends on the world, lightning storms blister the earth, for he
fears nothing, feels nothing, sees everything. From the beginning
he's been a juggernaut, crushing everything in his path, from the Hindi
Jagannath, Lord of the World, a guise of the god Vishnu. A dark
Lex Luthor was more what I was thinking of than Superman, ma'am.

Nick Carbó

ANG TUNAY NA LALAKI'S FOURTH WORKSHOP POEM
ASWANG VS WONDER WOMAN

From the ~~Wonder~~ invisible plane
Wonder Woman spots
~~a giant~~ big black bat wings fluttering

from window to window
along the upper west side
of Manhattan. This could be

the monster that's been sucking
live fetuses from pregnant mothers.
Wonder Woman dives

for a closer look, notices
~~it's just~~ it has a torso and two arms,
and a woman's head with long

black hair. She's eating something
fleshy and raw! Wonder Woman
gets on the radio, calls

the Justice League for back up.
It's too late, the *Aswang* is breaking
the glass of her cockpit. Aquaman

answers, "Sending the Green Lantern
and Hawkman. Over." The *Aswang*
has reached in, grabbed

the receiver from her hand
and its bloody ~~dog~~ canine teeth
ripping into Wonder Woman's

Wonder bracelet. She pushes the eject
button, catapults into the sky
to escape the ~~sharp~~ smelly *Aswang* teeth.

But Wonder Woman is not
out of it yet—the *Aswang* has
good radar, finds Wonder Woman

as she's falling, grabs
her by the legs and bites
into the golden boots.

Wonder Woman screams, "Let go!
You immigrant scum!" The *Aswang*
extends its claws,

"*Putang ina mo!* Yankee go
home!" Wonder Woman receives
gashes through her red, white,

and blue toga, "Speak English!
You foreign piece of crap! Ouch!"
The *Aswang* responds, "Eat my

bulbul you ugly American. And
have a nice trip!" letting go
of Wonder Woman's legs.

She is about to splat onto
Riverside Drive when a big fluffy
green baseball mitt appears

below her to break her fall.
"You're lucky I got here fast,"
Green Lantern says,

"And boy, you sure look
beat up." Wonder Woman searches
the sky, "When I get my

golden lasso around the neck
of that Filipino bitch monster,
I'll squeeze and never let go."

Hawkman is in pursuit
of the *Aswang*, chasing it under
elevated subway trains,

around the Chrysler building,
past the glowing tower
of the Empire State building.

Wonder Woman nurses her wounds
as she watches two sets of wings disappear
into dots above the New York sky line.

Krista Franklin

Platform, Position & Possibility: *Magneto Speaks*

We are gods. Our very thoughts could strip the axis from earth's belly, take continents apart like dismantled puzzles. Humans are a blight, plague of flesh swept through. To serve them is ignorance, casting pearls among swine. May the heavens collapse on them, their fear be the noose that slips around their puny necks. Nature has ordained our genes to speak the supernatural. It is only *this* we should obey.

I watched my family enter ovens, corralled like chattel to slaughter by these dogs. Do you think I will not destroy them? Legions of them stood while my wife shrieked inside a building of flames. I was trapped by them, their bodies, a wall that blocked me from her. The abrupt silence of her voice brought about their destruction.

I made a promise to her and her alone. The last one I will ever make. That night, I stepped over their carcasses buried beneath my wrath, and walked away from all of it. A large light bloomed inside me as their blood pooled at my feet. History has shown us who they are, that life is as valuable to them as trinkets from a candy machine. We were born to sweep them from this planet like dust.

Think of the possibilities.

Evan J. Peterson

SUPERVILLAINS

I am the Strange Charmer,
and I plan to rip out your quarks.

I am the Gluten Psychic,
the thought-rash consuming all.

I am the Ugliest Baby,
and you are required to hold me.

I am the CreMaster,
the millionaire muscle who will not be ignored.

I am the Power Slut.
I will seduce your honor student.

I am the Ultimate Man.
I don't even have an X chromosome.

I am the Queen of the Aether.
You do not exist until I imagine you.

I am Doctor Blastocyst,
zygotic despot of the Outer Womb.

I am the Phosphorous Phantom,
disintegrating all I illuminate.

I am Captain DirtyBomb,
and I have nothing left to lose.

I am the Avant-Cynic,
the only one left when evil becomes passé.

I am the PostVillain;
You only think you've seen it all.

Tim Seibles

Natasha in a Mellow Mood

apologies to Bullwinkle and Rocky

Boris, dahlink, look
at my legs, long
as a lonely evening in Leningrad,
how they open the air
when I walk, the way moonlight
open the dark. Boris, my hair
is so black with espionage,
so cool and quiet with all those secrets
so well kept—those secret plans
you've nearly kissed
into my ears. Who gives a proletarian
damn about Bullwinkle and that
flying squirrel and that idiot
who draws us? America
is a virgin, the cartoonist who leaves me
less than a Barbie doll under
this dress, who draws me
with no smell—**he** is a virgin.
The children who watch us
every Saturday mornink
are virgins. Boris, my sweet waterbug, I
don't want to be a virgin anymore.
Look into my eyes, heavy
with the absence of laughter
and the presence of vodka. Listen
to my Russian lips muss up
these blonde syllables of English:
Iwantchu. Last night
I dreamed you spelled your
code name on my shoulder
with the waxed sprigs of your
moustache. I had just come
out of the bath. My skin was still
damp, my hair poured like ink
as I pulled the comb through it. Then
I heard you whisper, felt you take

my hand—Oh, Boris, Boris
Badenov, I want your mischief-
riddled eyes to invent
my whole body, all the silken
slopes of flesh forgotten
by the blind cartoonist. I want
to be scribbled all over you
in shapes no pencil would dare. Dahlink,
why don't we take off
that funny little hat. Though
you are hardly tall
as my thighs, I want your pointy
shoes beside my bed, your
coat flung and fallen
like a double-agent
on my floor.

Tim Seibles

BORIS BY CANDLELIGHT

Natasha, first this—
then what? I'll be looking
into the shadows and, instead
of that buck-toothed squirrel, I'll see
your body drawn like an ivory blade
slicing the dark. Then what good
will I be to Fearless Leader?
All of Moscow will become your
slow walk, as though the entire city
swam with your slim thighs
shortening the streets.

Natasha, we are supposed to be
comrades in the struggle—we are
supposed to be taking the world
back from America. We should be nabbing
Rocky and giving him some convincing
bonks on the head. But don't think
I haven't noticed your blouse
ripe as midnight when you pass by
at headquarters, and that sleepy
invitation in your glance when
we've been spying too long
in the White House basement,
squinting into that small
circle of light.

Once I saw the wind turn around
in your raven hair and thought
of your dress as a full sail and
myself, a small island upon which you
might be shipwrecked for an evening.
Do you really think that when I
close my eyes it's Bullwinkle
that haunts the dim hall inside me?
But, dahlink, we are supposed to be

dreaming or a more perfect State.
You must understand, Natasha,
in every frame of this life
we invent ourselves and the air.
The cartoonist is just a sad rumor,
like the distance you see between us.

These lines that shape our bodies,
that separate us and break up the world—
they're there because you think
they're there. You have always been
a part of me, Natasha. I have
already sketched you a million times
with my soul's invisible ink.
I love you as much as I live
for Russia. But these capitalists,
baby, they will snatch even the broken moon
if we look away and let them.

Marta Ferguson

ORACLE REDIRECTS THE BULLET

You know that scene in *Buffy* where Warren
comes into the yard—gun-toting, shooting up
Buffy and, we see, delayed, Tara?

It's nothing new, Warren's just the joker
in the slayer's deck. Senseless as it was before.
When it was me.

Except that I'm in the chair and Willow?
Well, grief crazed and apocalyptic, but not
disabled. In my shoes, Red would mete it out.

Pop goes the world.

But me? I've adjusted. Life as a librarian
prepared me, I guess, to be less exciting.

If you believe that, come closer and
I'll show you what I've learned.

Collin Kelley

SECRET ORIGINS OF THE SUPER-VILLAINS

The comic book arrives in the mail,
found on eBay, sold by a stranger,
my childhood memory only $10 plus postage.
I've wanted this oversized DC since I was six,
cried over its disappearance
from the rack at Grant's,
my parents screaming at each other
over why they wasted money
on Lion Country Safari
when all I wanted was the comic:
Secret Origins of the Super-Villains.
The cover emblazoned on my brain,
a holy grail for almost thirty years:
Superman, Batman, The Flash,
and Wonder Woman all hard-charging
toward the enemies—Lex Luthor,
The Joker, Captain Cold and Cheetah.
Now I have it in my hands and it means nothing.
It's as perfect as a summer day in 1975,
unscarred by time, pristine in plastic.
Maybe I just want that year back,
and the twenty that followed.
To take those days, put them under
lock and key or on a high shelf,
protected from damage.
Maybe I just want to believe,
like when I was five,
that someone could save me.
Could keep my parents together,
save people from dying,
and buildings from falling.
Even at thirty-one, sitting in front of a TV
on a blue September morning
as the planes crashed in NYC,
I held out hope there might be a Superman.

Jay Snodgrass

CLOWN FACE

The milk washes like flesh over Formica
until it is transparent,
but the concrete is soft, like in a dream
where I visited the carnival
and was dropped into the water
at the dunking stand,

how the ripples of water became
denuded faces radiating out,
reflecting, cutting away density.

In the streets I became the heart-bomb
innocently carried in a suitcase.
I was almost near giving that up
when I decided to turn the hospital
and parking garage to fried ampersands
of grease & gravy.

Let me tell you my ancestry is a mixed boat,
not mixed but ordained
to come as funeral makeup & wax;
to be carried,
upon death, through the door in suitcases.

I'm charred to remember you.
Dear.

Raymond McDaniel

THE PERSISTENCE OF ESPIONAGE

Chameleon Boy rides the maglev to Montauk,
nobody on that train, its bare tremble
socialist, synthetic slide down the future,
its dead white world's fair.
Empty stations, empty agents—
no more buttons, no more coats.
Reep Daggle dreams of Durla, her imagine ocean,
her drowned city neither coral nor spire.
Its epics are a collective colossus,
generations beached and bleached,
over two hundred tons of elegant elbow
sunk in diatomaceous sand, fallen body
of friend and foe and family,
right angle of the wrist risen to vertigo.
In the last exploit of the Espionage Squad,
all the useless heroes will die
except Chameleon Boy, his neural net
polyform and plasticene, eternal.
But yes, Phantom Girl, Shrinking Violet,
Invisible Kid. A lost city looms
behind the wrecked and ruined dunes.
Forty thousand colors, eighty thousand ages.
The world is not like this at all.

Evan J. Peterson

DESIRE. ENDLESS.

after Elissa Ball's "Holy Haiku"

I am abstinence cracking
      & discretion swept under rugs.

I am the hungry ghosts
      & the feet they've lost in the river.

I am the moral paralysis of a shame culture.

I am a burqa of bandages.
      I am medical couture.

I am the prettiest horse.

I am fetishes so precise
      they have no website.

I am the leather interior,
      the luxury as head-on collision
folds your knees into your chest.

I am the junk needle
      in the voice of the rock star
& the prayer
      that he won't grow too old.

I am the spice drug in the throat
      of the sandworm, the lengths
you'll go to get it.

I am Captain America
      assassinated.

I am the unnecessary fact
      that every Dr. Who is reincarnated
as a white dude.

I am the awkward girl
hidden in a TARDIS costume.

I am the obese man dressed
          as Catwoman. Why?

Because *fuck you,*
          that's why.

I am Patrick Stewart
          charging $75 per autograph.
(Has he nothing else to do on a Sunday?)

I am Adam West, aging.
          I am Gillian Anderson, aging.
I am Carrie Fisher: *Unable to attend.*

I am Wil Wheaton & the need
          to stalk Wil Wheaton.

I am not Love. Jesus is Love.
          My reach extends much farther.

Nor am I the Devil; He makes deals.

I am every item on everyone's list
          of dealbreakers.

I am the not-pleasure,
          the not-getting,
& I don't grant wishes.

I'm the bitch that every song's about
          & *I don't wanna be friends—*

I want your eyes to turn goldgreen
       & see only me.

I want your shoulders to sag,
       but only slightly.

I want your bended knees
       & upturned palms.
I want all the teeth in your head
       on a string around my neck.

All I want from you is everything.
       What more is there to want?

Bryan D. Dietrich

KRYPTON NIGHTS

If I could leave my shadow only
behind, the air my body displaced
these many years, the suggestion
of water, night sweat, where just, say,
a cheekbone was before…. Dread. Even
that I would bequeath you if I could.

Yet, if you've received this, remember
tall sticks planted in the ground at noon.
No, remember there is no this. No
me. No reader, no last planetary
observer. No journal, no witness,
no conclave, no revival, no grand

revolution, no susurration,
no sea to come from, no sun to return
to, no Krypton days, no Krypton nights.
Only charmed figments of electric
residue. This ghost of light, pulse,
silence. Binary diaspora. This me

who I am not but will be soon, if only
briefly, until you turn toward your own
pale sun, the focus shifts, the quality
of light changes, and the shadow you
yourself cast grows shorter or longer
and you find that you've found another

me, and through me, another fragment
of who I may suggest, and soon have
constructed a vast history of, well, your own.
Still, for a civilization of one
its anatomy is just as real as you
were when I touched you, entered, reemerged.

This, then, is the power of knowing, this death.
When the last Krypton night simmers over
the rim of your world, when we meet in the sky
to find ourselves sharing stars, when what was
once familiar slinks away, disoriented,
hungry for the next clarity, remember

shadows cast from nothing in the dark.

Lucille Clifton

if i should

to clark kent

enter the darkest room
in my house and speak
with my own voice, at last,
about its awful furniture,
pulling apart the covering
over the dusty bodies; the randy
father, the husband holding ice
in his hand like a blessing,
the mother bleeding into herself
and the small imploding girl,
i say if i should walk into
that web, who will come flying
after me, leaping tall buildings?
you?

Michael Martone

THE SEX LIFE OF THE FANTASTIC FOUR

INVISIBLE GIRL

Where he touches me, I vanish. The back of his hand stroking my face erases my cheek. Involuntary, the skin initially, then the deeper flesh. The skin first, gone when it feels his fingertips. I feel the surface disappear but still feel feeling there. His touch sinks in. The subdermal layers go. The nested cells he polishes clear, his soft palm hovering. By the time I have stripped off the blue bodysuit, stepping out of the spandex which retains, for a second, the shape of my body as it falls, the body it reveals has already become translucent, the meat turning milky, the bone wiped clear in streaks like a smear of butter melts the white from a paper plate. I become clarified grease beneath him. Entwined, we are tangled up in the skein of my airy sinew, the ropey braids of my circulatory system, its cartoon of primary reds and blues. My blood thins in the extremities but knots at the nodes of erectile tissue, clotting a nipple visible again beneath the sheen he has left from licking what looked, a moment before, like air, now, me, there, concentrated into rubbery ruby light again. It disappears into his mouth. I am down to the broken dashes of the central nervous system, suggesting, still outlining, the outer neural net of my skin, feeding me the synaptic code of dots and dits from the dissipating periphery. His hands, as they caress nothing, reveal me to myself, leave the afterimage of his movement burned upon the transparent wall of my retina, the lightning streak of his skin shaping the borders of my own body. I close my eyes and watch as my eyelids dissolve. My vision passes through skin first, turning then to scrim. And I see, now, through another unoccluded lens. I see through my lids, through myself, see his cock, clearly, moving inside of the vast and now empty empty space which must be me and must be not me.

THE HUMAN TORCH

I sit at the bar, usually, drinking ouzo neat, a Jordan almond dissolving at the bottom of the shot glass. I have set the liquor on fire swizzling it with my finger. I like to watch the floor show and the show on the floor. The tunnel crowd weirded-out by the drag queens doing strip teases or singing old torch songs "One for my baby and one more for the road," sending up Lady Day or Barbra, that kind of thing. I dump some water into my aperitif extinguishing the blue flame and turning the drink chalky like a precipitate in a test tube. My current favorite is a Liza interpreter who vamps this obscure number—is it by Mercer?—which plays with the line, "You've let yourself go." She sings to her lug of a lover how he had grown fat and dull, how their liaison has suffered the consequences. There follows a litany of complaint. What a schlub, she sings. "You've let yourself go." But it turns in the end. It always turns. "Come on over here," she whispers, "come on over and let yourself go." I tear up, naturally, but it isn't saline staining my cheek. It's a dab of molten lava percolating there in the corner of my eye, my own brand of running mascara. I have to watch myself. Spontaneously, my eyelashes can ignite, throwing sparks up into the tinder of my eyebrows which can smoulder for hours without my knowing. Once, I set the sprinklers off in the Russian Bath House on 10th. I've stopped looking for a boy who can top me. It's too dangerous. The leather bars. Too hot. I was cooking inside the horsehide Eisenhower jacket, cooking the jacket, the seared meat smell an additional turn-on, I suppose. These powers we have acquired seem to fall into that dark space between the involuntary responses wired into us and those we can modulate. Not like the heartbeat on the one hand or walking home on the other, but like blinking and winking, say, or like desire itself. There is only so much one can do to help oneself. Oh sure I can bellow "Flame On" all I want followed by the stunning transformation from solid buff flesh to superheated gaseous vapor. The controlled burn. Here precision scalding. There the delicate sweating of copper pipes. But in the weaker moments, when I am weak in the knees, a stranger's hand on my hand will steam off skin. I can't watch myself all the time. A human touch sets off the human torch. I am a captive within my sublime hide.

MR. FANTASTIC

To make the edge of the famous samurai swords of antiquity, the smiths beat the iron flat into foil then folded the metal over and hammered it flat again. And then another fold and peening, and still another and then another. Thousands of times. Fold and flatten, fold and flatten. Until, in this primitive way, through brute force and patience, the metal's crystalline structure became saturated with itself. Atoms packed inside the spaces between atoms, at last, both the surface and simultaneously its underside now no more than a molecule deep, the edge of the matrix serrated only by the minute undulation of subatomic matter, a sine wave, spanning a mere handful of angstroms, of the outermost electrons. Sharp, you bet. It is what I find myself doing to my own skin in private moments. I stretch and fold and knead it back together. A wrinkle in the loose hide on my forearm, a flap of fat at my chin. It is the very definition of definition, and I spend hours honing my musculature, ironing in the pleats on my belly, increasing the cant of my cheekbones with the finest shade of a sharpened pencil line. I know what people are thinking. The elasticity of your normal everyday run-of-the-mill uncosmically irradiated penis is, itself, a goddamn miracle to most. The ways it inflates, its skin thinning to the gauziest of tissue webbed by diaphanous capillary sponge grown thick with the stiffened rebar of packed and interlocking corpuscles. Sure, I've tried it all. Swallowed myself whole, took myself in myself from behind. For awhile she liked to watch it snake toward her across the floor, liked the way it coiled up a leg then threaded the cleft of her rear, whipping around her waist then back up her back, curling over her shoulder and back down between her breasts down her stomach, parting her down down there and then her labia and into her from above, how its tensile strength lifted her in this hardened harness, held her weightless as it expanded within her and all around her. We haven't done that in awhile, and everything, believe me, grows familiar. Recently our lovemaking has tended toward the less baroque. A simple vertical embrace, my member remembering its scale from before the accident. Sue, her legs wrapped around my waist, is saddled on my hips, riding this altogether unfantastic appendage and me supporting her, strapping my silly, pliant arms around her, then around me and then around her again. Stretching, another lap and lapping another lap, another band around us both, belting us to us. My arms still encircling, encasing us from head to toe, this cocoon spinning while we kiss, my elasticity nearing its end, effaced to the point of transparency, my thinning skin becoming, at last, the clear outer covering, at last, of this new creature we create.

THE THING

I don't really need the briefs down below since my thing ain't there no more. It's more for show to let the folks know I was once a guy. A scrap of cloth for the modesty of the citizens craning their necks to take a gander at me. They can't get past the orangey crust of skin. It's something all right. Little do they know I am all hanging out there for anybody to see. My Johnson, or that I take to by my Johnson (Johnsons really—I don't know since there is no other thing like me, as far as I can tell, to let me try out these doohickeys of wadded callous and thingamabobs of oozing mucus) is plopped there in front of their collective noses. Just more eruptions and rashes on the sliding plates of my scaly surface. The Doc explained it to me, showed me the Tinkertoy models of your typical twisted normal gene, and then how mine's been tripled, another worm squirming around that ladder of goofy golf balls. It's simple for everybody but me. Male and female. Male and female down to everybody's bones but me. No bones for me. No in and out. No on and off. A whole other dimension to nookie. What I have become needs a couple other things to reproduce, I guess, not just one other. Sex, as near as I can figure, is like nothing you can dream of since those dirty pictures your brain's pumping out are made up of, you got it, those same twin strands caught wrapped up in each other. Well, I am another other. And I am on the lookout for other others like me. Meantime, when I'm alone (but this could be in the middle of Times-freaking-Square, a public spectacle where the public can't begin to see the me that's me) I make myself have this nameless thing, feel this Thing thing I have no words, no more, for.

C. R. Resetarits

CRISIS ON INFINITE EARTHS

Flash, the Atom, Green Lantern,
and their conflicting
storylines
from barstool to booth
and back again.

Superman checking his
Kandor at the door,
while age and angles
are Robin's crisis, his desire
to ever-be someone's wonder boy.

And then there's Doll Man
wandering in and out
of conversations or well-lit reflections
stuck and struck by the wonders
of his delicate six-inch persona.

Multiverse fixes,
interdimensional crosses,
infinite takes on origins and powers
and pick-up lines between
happy and zero hour.

Playing at mystery most
Monday nights under the influence
of kryptonite or dollar beer
at Jake's Dilemma between
west 80 and west 81st.

Alan King

X-MEN

for Truth Thomas and the students at Homewood

Drew's battling in the Danger Cave.
His rhymes are retracting metal claws he swings
at holograms that lunge at him.
Disappointments are collapsing walls
he backflips to avoid. Sometimes I wonder
if you have to be an acrobat
to survive America. The way she treats me
I might as well have an X-gene.
Just the other day, when a police cruiser
followed me for several blocks,
my heart was a speaker with the bass
turned up. Sweat beads popped out
like the heads of nosy neighbors.
Like the students at Homewood,
I wish I could teleport out of those moments
or shape-shift to a human.
Truth says they need what we bring them
every Tuesday, and I remember his ruby quartz
battle visor glowing when he emits his wisdom:
This world is fucked up, but it don't have to stay that way.
The optic blast in their minds has incandescent stanzas
shooting out of Bryan when he kicks his verse,
while Amelia levitates verses
in the telekinetic air.

Christopher Hennessy

BATMAN'S ADDRESS, OR THE THEORY OF FORT KNOX

It will never be safe, Superfriends.
The Legion of Doom is always already
escaping in their skull-shaped rocket ship,
always just fast enough to out-run the Invisible Jet
and even Superman and the Flash.
The loot is heavy in the hold.
And still they zoom into their swamp.

We are not who we think we are.
Look in their eyes, Lex's deep, seductive
onyx, the ragged black holes of the Scarecrow,
the zombie gaze of Solomon Grundy—can't you see it?
Can't you see it in the way they lick their lips? Grod
the Gorilla, a genius eating bananas with his feet.

Watch them as they crowd into their skull,
their foreheads nearly touching as they plan
their next heist, seated, suddenly like presidents,
at their Roundtable of Doom.

We are the soft, hidden and heavy gold bars
the enemy desires. We are the ray guns
they steal every other week, the very theory
of might-makes-right Lex bangs out, his manly
fists never once splintering his tiny podium.

Admit your face, too, etched angular
where it should be soft, blunted chin
where it should be jutted in heroism.

Save the kitten from the tree
and make love to your doppelgänger
and give up the tights, for god's sake,
give up the tights and peace will reign.

Raymond McDaniel
"The Menace of Dream Girl"
Adventure Comics #317, February 1964

Saturn Girl's a stickler for protocol

she summons all far-flung Legionnaires for meeting

calling all Legionnaires, she's a re-minder

so we sit and sit still

for readings of the Constitution

(clause 6 sub-clause 3 requires that every Legionnaire use

language learning machines to blah blah)

Mon-El maintains perfect posture

Triplicate Girl nearly falls asleep

finally the new applicants arrive

SIZZLING SUNS!

that Dream Girl's dreamy all right!

the boys go all googly, so *thank God for Saturn Girl*

prissy, proper, impatient

"I'm *sorry*, but *dreaming* isn't a *super*power"

but the boys, smitten, sweaty, overrule her

and Nura dreams TERRIBLE MENACE:

eggs that hatch reeking beasts

Metropolis Spaceport blown to bits

When the vote comes it falls along gender lines

yea boys and nay ladies

but crises wait not for courting

the iron curtain of time

persists but by now Dreamy's an unmanageable bitch

she mission-accompanies Lightning Lass, who "somehow"

loses her powers

It doesn't stop there, either

Dream Girl's read the rules rightly

she's suddenly Clause Queen

speaking Law French and all those stupid subclauses

she takes us out one by one

she uses the Vondra Aurora to turn us into superinfants.

who knows what motivates pretty people

but the boys are surely sore about it now
yet it turns out Nura had dreamed an unclear dream

she saw us die and sought to save us

(for how can harm come to Legionnaires-no-longer?)

in the end it's a compromise

sorry for the confusion, she says

won't you reapply, Star Boy asks

and Dream Girl says *maybe later*.

But she's *Dream Girl*. She *knew*

even then. Unfair, her future

that once was ours.

Alan King

DREAMS OF COMIC BOOK WOMEN

after Lyrae Van Clief-Stefanon

Give me everything I can touch:
What's round: What speeds
the blood: What raises the drawbridge:
What will fit on my tongue:
A hunger rising like thought bubbles.

The dreams are bright colors—
even at 16, waking to the promise of Betty and Veronica,
I wanted to be Archie,
caught between glossy mouths
like strawberry shortcakes.

Storm's battle suit swallowed her body
the way a boy gobbles a chocolate bar.
What I lick off my fingers, dreaming of a perfect world
where everything can be touched without consequences.

I dream of sweet things: the tempting glaze of a strudel,
the moist center of an apple croissant; or waking to Madame Hydra,
Catwoman and Mystique mistaking me for icing,
a melting popsicle, ice cream running down a waffle cone.

Give me the assassin, Elektra, in her Twizzler-colored suit
hanging as if someone attempted to rip it off her.
Let my appetite for sweets keep me dreaming through the wars
and unemployment. Let me go on like Ulysses' men, dazed
and wandering—never dreaming of home.

meg eden

pantoum for expired cosplayers

we wait in the city in line, dressed
like our childhood idols: capes, wands,
as we speak in theater-outside voices, "Give me
sushi rice and obento with careful hands."

like our childhood idols: capes, wands
make us believe we have attained divinity.
sushi, rice and obento, with careful hands,
passed as we sit on the pavement, considering what

makes us believe we have attained divinity.
is this a universally human desire, or perhaps exclusive? dreams
passed as we sit on the pavement, considering what
bearded men in sailor dresses desire—

is this a universally human desire, or perhaps exclusive: to dream
as we speak in theater-outside voices, "Give me
bearded men in sailor dresses, desire—"
we wait in the city in line, dressed.

Dane Cervine

THE FANTASTIC FOUR

After the phone call with my three siblings,
I remember our childhood, the four of us pretending
to be The Fantastic Four superheroes from Marvel comics:
Stretcho, the Invisible Girl, her brother the Torch,
their rock-man friend The Thing. Each imbued with a gift—
elasticity, invisibility, fire, strength. My two brothers,
my sister and I, perfect incarnations of this quartet
as we'd run the sidewalks confronting the hidden villains
of quiet suburban streets. Looming in the distance,
the adult world of parents sagging onto couches at day's end,
wistfully lingering over Ray Charles'
Take These Chains From My Heart.
It was a world only the brave could face,
which we did, slowly transmogrifying
into the adult heroes we wanted to become.
As now: phone cradled, silent,
mother's stroke menacing our horizon,
but the telepathy still working,
the call springing us into action—
an invisible force-field to bind us, together,
in flame, the irreducible strength of stone,
the heart stretching, stretching.

Jason Mott

AN OPEN LETTER TO UP AND COMING WORLD-SAVERS
Wonder Woman

We all know the keys to our own transformations:
the secluded phone booths, the darkened caves,
the candlesticks that open the secret changing room
in the library, the magic words that conjure lightning,

and on and on. We've all created our methods
of shedding self in favor of the Freud's superego.
And while the formulaic dangers persist—the villains
shambling over the landscape in their giant robots,

launching into their fits of egomania, their grand soliloquies
protesting their underappreciated intelligence or perhaps
just their general discontent at whatever plot twist
was written into their lives and broke their will

to resist the Id—while all of these persist,
both the superhero and the superego are blessed.
This is the time of logic, of well-defined conclusions,
of rising action, climactic battle, predictable outcome.

This is the time when the hero can honestly say "I exist."
But then the dust settles. The arch nemesis is taken away—
until the next scheduled escape—the fires are outed,
the busted buildings cordoned off and scheduled

for later resurrection, the survivors reunited with the arms
of whomever they called out for as the world was crashing
down. And the dead, even they are given their proper
placement in the gardens of our memory.

But then, what of the heroes? Dressed in the glamour
of their gilded getup with no one left to save, with nothing left
to do but return to their practiced fictions: a newspaper reporter,
an aloof billionaire, a teacher, a policeman,

a soldier, a poet, whatever it is they were before
the cape and the double-edged promises that are woven
into the fabric of such things. The heroes, they stretch
and bend and tear at the seams of their existence

trying to fill the shadow left by those noble, mythological
alternative selves; trying to remain, for a little while longer
more of the "Super" than of the "man," more of the "Wonder"
than the "woman." But night invariably comes.

The costume always sullies and the outer skin
must inevitably be removed. To those aspiring
to be rescuers, those hoping to be the hands of salvation
for someone at any cost, I offer this advice:

console the mirror first. Because, more than any death
rays, more than any mad scientist or extra-dimensional
overlord yearning for conquest and power, more than
a storyline cancellation, more than a wounded heart,

it is the dissonance that kills.

Stephen Burt

LITTLE LAMENT FOR THE LEGION OF SUPER-HEROES

Too many to list, but we recognized them all
Among each issue's battles: Saturn Girl
Wore white and red; read minds; once quit the team
And let her teenage colleagues try to save
The 30th century from shape-shifters, ghosts,
Illusionists whose eyes ate through the page.

Without his armor on, sad Wildfire
Was nothing but a bright electric blur;
His flashy powers weighed less on his mind
Than flesh or blood he lacked. Shrinking Violet
Hid safe below a fight, then, from beneath
A villain's notice, would grow up so fast
One punch as she arose laid bad guys low.

On covers, in collectors' see-through bags,
In close-formation flight (like kites, like geese)
Arrayed for fans to find and name each one,
We knew you by your logos, stripes and capes;
You knew how long we wished we could dispel
What we were called at home—the middle-school
Kingdom of terms clapped on us like applause,
Which, fastening on us, tell us we serve,
And let our powers go...
                                        The future's kids
Could name themselves: a wish under whose laws
The powers to burn metals like small suns
And to make one's own body helium
Are the same gift—the talent equally
Of winged Dawnstar; magnetic Cosmic Boy
And Matter-Eater Lad; Braniac Five;
Chameleon Boy. Light Lass. Star Boy. Dream Girl.

Nicholas Allen Harp

X-MEN

Today in the School for Gifted Youngsters Xavier's lesson plan calls
for sex education, the hows and whos, wheres and whens dispensed
delicately, his bald brow furrowed serious, his students wide-eyed,
chuckling, unabashedly alive and constantly, at risk from you-name-it:
G-men, invasive telepathy, Plutonian radiation, slack-jawed villains,
and now, he can't believe it, gonorrhea, pregnancy, AIDS, each
contemporary malady less innocent than the one before, a curriculum
chock-full of acronymic woe and code—IUD, HIV, RU-486—too many
physical choices in the modern world, Xavier thinks, too many forces
stitching lifeforce inextricably to doomed youth, their piss and vinegar
mutated into glowy juice, concussion orbs, optic blasts, blizzards
summoned by sheer merge of will, their bodies already breaking out
from under themselves, pushing and yanking their skins like the
colleague they call Fantastic, their young lives catapulted into flight
(*literally*, he thinks, *flight*) to some fate he cannot, despite his infamous
prescience, predict, a factored variable he'll have to follow, patiently,
like a serial; the X of a xenophobic country, lonesome Xmases,
x ratings, the x's and o's he'll send his students when he expels them
to the dangerous world.

D.A. Powell

[MY NECK A TOOTHSOME FEEDING GROUND. VESPERED SWARMS HAD DRUNK OF ME BEFORE THIS NEW BATMAN]

a song of Robin

don't be fooled by costumes: I am still an orphan.   I move through his house by stealth.   I thieve.
he won't last: when he kisses I'll pull away.   already I know the short attention span of my body

my neck a toothsome feeding ground.   vespered swarms had drunk of me before this new batman

down every dark corridor of gotham I seek my next guardian.   capes fly open: how hunger rushes

when I'm ready to be circled one will circle.   secret cave.   I can make his voice bounce back
boy wonder.   he will believe he is the one hero.   I must remember to wince when I feel his fangs

Jason McCall

Sidekick Funeral: Jason Todd

Don't ask what we want;
We will always want
blood, a few young necks
offered to wet our cracked lips.
How many Greeks dreamed
of Iphigenia's neck?
Whose face followed Pilate from Galilee
to Gaul? You

never got used to the grave, did you?
We felt the earth moving
when we left you flowers.
Resurrection is a part our world.
That was our excuse. Of course,
we knew you'd come back as a hero or hood,
shade or angel—a reminder
of how mean men can be
when god gives us a life
and lets us decide how it should end.

Michael Kriesel

SUPERBOY ROBOTS

Like a blob or the Borg, I absorb my
girlfriend's memories of playing Barbie,
then extract a few lives from her cat, Mr. Biggles.
Sunday's a buffet of faces at the grocery store.
Fixing on a person, place or thing, I suck its soul
out through its nose, like some nostril Nosferatu.
Red squirrels mummify, become dried apples.
Lawns leach white. I visualize time as transparent
sand, and throw handfuls of it at things
to get them where they're going faster.
Certain people don't age well around me.
I'm the child in Whitman's poem, assimilating
lilacs, riverbanks…gulping down the dawn,
becoming something larger than myself.

Here's what really happened: I joined the navy.
Slept with men and women. Drank like a fish.
Smoked like a dragon. Swore like a parrot.
Got divorced and married. Helped raise
a girlfriend's daughter for a couple years—
then left. Celibate as a tree, I live alone,
writing and chanting and lifting, my higher
self descending to inhabit me like Clark Kent
in math class, who can't always save us,
so he has a closet of Superboy robots.
They extinguish fires and foil bank robbers
while the real boy of steel's stuck in school
or busy banging Lois Lane, or too hung over to fly.
My closet door rattles some nights, but it's locked.

Lucille Clifton

note passed to superman

sweet jesus, superman,
if i had seen you
dressed in your blue suit
i would have known you.
maybe that choirboy clark
can stand around
listening to stories
but not you, not with
metropolis to save
and every crook in town
filthy with kryptonite.
lord, man of steel,
i understand the cape,
the leggings, the whole
ball of wax.
you can trust me,
there is no planet stranger
than the one i'm from.

Marc Pietrzykowski

BUCKY, NEAR INFIRM FROM YEARS UNDERGROUND, RESURFACES TO VISIT THE DEATHBED OF CAPTAIN AMERICA

You got sick and I heard and came
and found all the vegetables
rotted in the fridge. The scene was holy:
the neighbors' chimes clanging,
eggplant deflated and furry...
It was just beautiful. You got sick

and everyone prayed and there was
time to pray. You got sick enough
to make them all believe it.

Well, good for you. The flowers
from the Falcon
cloyed, I left them in the bedpan.
When you were so sick I confess

I wished a time or two you'd just die,
and then, when you stopped being sick, well,

not a good joke. Your forehead—
the battles, the years beaten into it.
You, never a jokester, not a card or ham,
and sure not so funny this time—
and then all jokes stopping together.

I bagged groceries for thirty-five
years at your request, came running, found:
your ears pursed in fungusy pouches,
eyes blank and piggy, sharpened to points.
How is it you, old man, fought Red Skull
all those years just to give in,
just to swap your shield
for a seaside room and meals
in the commons?

No matter.
All the holes are sewn or pressed
shut now. Might be
you are fighting still,
but not here. Not with us that need it.

Jason Mott

A SONG FOR HEALERS

Bruce Wayne, for Alfred

The two of us spent that first night hung, tied
to one another. You said that I should learn

to remember the summer winds, the hide-
and-seek games with Mother, Father's well-earned

reputation for strength and forgiveness.
Ultimately, the memories that stayed

wore a gunman's shape. They held, like a mist
on a glass lake, to the man that was made

from blood so long ago. You tried to clean
it all away, but I tattooed the dead

to my thin wrists. Their ink has stained my dreams
and their faces clutter inside my head.

　　I can't stitch up the wound I am, and fight
　　to see why you would mend me every night.

Bruce Boston

CURSE OF THE SUPERHERO'S WIFE

That knee-length cape.
Those ridiculous leotards.
The bodysuit with its garish colors,
its moronic monogram insignia
emblazoned like a burning bush
upon his pumped-up pecs.

She has lost count of the times
she has washed and ironed
—mended and altered!—
the entire ghastly ensemble
so he can appear sleek and clean
before his legions of adoring fans.

The forgotten dinner parties.
The vacations canceled as they
are about to board the plane.
The way he will often vanish
in the middle of an evening
when friends come to call.

She has long since lost track
of the hundreds of excuses
she has had to make for him,
the pack upon passel of stories
she has been forced to concoct
and elaborate on his behalf.

The forty-odd hours or more
she must slave away each week
so they can afford the payments
on a tacky house in a tacky city
where crime and rape and havoc,
oblivious to his daring escapades,
continue to flourish like weeds.

All of this—the sweat, the lies,
the toil, the tears!—to preserve
his ever-so-precious anonymity,
the sacred secret of his identity.

Oh the secrets *she* could tell!
She could expose his boundless
vanity, how he couch-potatoes
the newscasts, awaiting any
mention of his lurid exploits,
how he leers at passing women
in the street—some of them
barely teenage girls—literally
undressing them with his eyes.

She could talk about his bouts
of depression and the Halcion,
deliver the lowdown on a super
hero's idea of super sex: forked
lightning foreplay, an equally
rapid-fire finale, and as a fitting
denouement, thunder-bumper
snores that rattle the windows
in their frames and drive her
downstairs to toss and turn
on the sprung living-room sofa.

Yet each time she considers revealing
his identity and his boots of clay,
every time she begins to calculate
the revenue—six figures at least!—
his overdue exposure might demand,
as she reaches for the telephone,
she recalls the look of menace
that can break like a bomb cloud
across his boyishly handsome face,

she thinks of the bruises he leaves
on her arms, on her back and thighs,
without even trying, she remembers
the touch of his hands like steel traps!

"History makes heroes of fools,"
some ancient sage once quipped.
"Heroes," another pundit claimed,
"are always boring in the end."

And what of superheroes?
And what of the accursed wives
of such ostentatious jackanapes?

Questions she often ponders
as she lets the phone slip back
into its cradle, as she once more
takes up her needle and thread.

Harry Man

J. JONAH JAMESON

Miss Brown!! This is Godzilla-huge.
Vacations are for simps and weaklings.

Buying all that old S.H.I.E.L.D. junk surplus was genius!
The cops wanted to quarantine us both because of that bomb.

How about trying on a good old-fashioned left cross!
I see it all now, Marla, you've joined with the others.

The younger generation's going to the dogs!
The older generation too, might as well blast everyone!

Slander is spoken, in print it's libel.
For $300 a day I'm shelling out, I'll do anything I feel like!

I told you to take pictures of kids in Halloween costumes.
All I see are shots of that show-off, Spider-Man!

He's probably out stealing hubcaps somewhere!
Empty-headed teenagers, they're all alike!

No more masks and no more excuses about creepy secret identities.
You'd think those simpletons would thank me for giving them a salary,

oh, I've seen their accusing eyes whenever I walk into editorial.
Ah, my beloved constituents, how I adore basking in their approval.

I picked up the wall-crawler and carried him away.
No one's a hero every day of the week.

Parker did anyone ever tell you that you're a pumpkin head?
Now you get out of here kid, you bother me.

Barbara Hamby

OLIVE OYL THINKS ABOUT QUANTUM THEORY

Oh, I can hear you laughing now. That permanent post-nasal drip,
Queen of Saturday Morning—what can she know about math or
science? You'd be surprised. I got straight As when I was at
Ubu Roi High School and Regional Dada Institute. My friend, Bev,
went to raves, smoked pot on the corner. Not me. Forget about sex.
You can guess the kind of guys a skinny gal attracts. Buzz
Abercrombie was my lab partner. We built an atomic bomb,
can you believe it, for our senior project. Our teacher plotzed,
even though it was just on paper, and I did more than my half,
going to the lab every weekend from October until March.
I had a ball at the prom. The music was funky, the deejay
kept playing "Shotgun" by Junior Walker over and over until
midnight. I danced till I disappeared, or so it's seemed since then.

Lynn Schmeidler

ANOTHER WORD FOR SKY IS UPSIDE-DOWN-UNDERSTORY

Sheena Queen of the Jungle
I get you—
you don't know how to act
around men,
but you can throw
a bamboo spear like nobody
ever orphaned you.

Your aura is electric green,
you straddle
moss-dripped limbs
in leopard-print minis,
bubble out of your pelt bra
like steamed cream on a café au lait.
You ride zebras!

Sit your fiercely-proficient-
in-knife-fighting self
over here,
and give me something
I can use. Surprise me
like you do
your enemies.

O lady of the jungle,
I ranked you
99th in *100 Sexiest Females
of All Time,*
And like you, I prefer to be alone
with my clench and dispossession.
I, too, speak with animals.

What if there were someone
to tell us
not to pick our teeth
with arrowheads?
We heroines have to stick together
in a casual but amazing way
like an archipelago.

Chris Bullard

SIDEKICK

In fifth grade every afternoon
I'd bicycle to Merritt's mother's
bungalow to sit splay legged
next to Merritt while we read
the latest comic book issues
from a collection sprawling over
the bedroom floor like the pages
of some immense encyclopedia
broken loose from its bindings,
passing each other the best images
as we commented on the superheroes, who broke through walls,
solved intricate crimes, caught
villains in beams from their rings,
and sped faster than any enemy.
I liked the explosions in big letters,
the skewed science, the plot lines
in which the hero was almost
destroyed, but hung on to win.
We talked about who was stronger,
smarter, more of a freak, most likely
to die, most alone: Clark Kent
in his icy Fortress of Solitude,
or wealthy Bruce Wayne brooding
over Gotham City in his mansion
above the Bat Cave. Superheroes,
we agreed, were, by necessity, loners.
Friends, family, wives would only
be dragged along like house trailers
hitched to sports cars. Loved ones
would ask too many questions
and, if they were harmed, would
cause a superhero too much pain.
Even Wonder Woman, Merritt's
favorite, never really hung out
with the other Amazons. All

a hero needed was a good sidekick:
some wise-cracking cub reporter
or a gruff mechanic who kept
the super gear mission-ready.

Merritt's mother tried to be cheerful
around me, but once she let me in
she would disappear like a chief
who had given one of his secret
agents an impossible assignment.
She once told me I was a good influence
on Merritt. I wasn't sure if I wanted
to be an influence on anyone, least
of all Merritt, who, when we went out
for cherry Coke floats and the boys
at the drugstore called him a sissy,
fought back by bending his fingers
into claws and hissing at them.
"C'mon," I'd say, "Let's go read
some comics," and pull him back
before he got creamed. Merritt
never took down a bully. He
never read aloud a personal essay
that brought everyone to hugs.
That wasn't the last panel. Mostly,
Merritt cried through class, more
and more, until his mom pulled him
out of school. I never knew why
the other boys rode Merritt so hard.
I never knew why I came over
to sit with Merritt every afternoon.
Maybe—I just wanted to learn how
Merritt endured, just as I wanted
to know what bravery was and how
a superhero should conduct himself
in the dangerous world. So when

I biked home with this stubby kid
who said the other boys thought
I was a jerk for not trying out
for the team and keeping to myself,
I could only think that a sidekick
always stays a sidekick and never
turns into one of the henchmen, even
when a superhero leaves this world
and can't say why or for how long he'll be gone.

Ned Balbo

THE CRIMEFIGHTER'S APPRENTICE

ABC-TV's Batman television series, ca. 1966;
for my adoptive father Carmine

He'd seen his parents die, crowd ordered back. He'd watched them fall,
the trapeze split and dangling, Big Top black after they fell.

The tragedy disguised by costumes, comics, TV show
remained the core of who he was. Don't look. He'd watched them fall.

Pale blanket knotted at the neck, I, too, would wear a mask,
wrestling my weary father, home from work. "Pretend to fall!"

The narrative obscure, no villain rose to challenge us—
no one clothed in a question mark would mock us as we fell.

Cliffhangers split in two for broadcast on successive nights
trapped heroes in the first half. What bad luck had made them fall?

Risk-takers, they had stumbled, dangling at the same abyss
that swallowed up their parents. World gone dark, they, too, would fall—

Next night, *deus ex machina* extracted from a belt
saved Bat and Acolyte: Houdini-like, they'd never fall.

My father never got the jokes—neither did I, too young—
But still he watched, a good sport, feigning shock when villains fell.

Perhaps the sum of who we are equals one moment's grief
held back and multiplied, a chalkline mark where bodies fell.

The memory of loss, of murder, hides behind a mask...
How did the saboteur escape? He struck, two people fell—

And yet, the boy would choose the colors not of night but day,
both thrush and legendary thief. Grim joke? He'd watched them fall.

But, deadened, he'd seen something else: merciless gravity
undone by triple-spins in flight, Fate tricked when no one fell.

Note: "The Crimefighter's Apprentice" makes use of artist Bob Kane and collaborator Bill Finger's 1939 comic-book creation (Robin was introduced in 1940) and ABC's 1966-68 half-hour television series which aired twice weekly (on Wednesday and Thursday nights) to accommodate its cliffhanger structure.

Pat M. Kuras

DICK GRAYSON

Oh, Starfire was never
right for you,
you of the short pants
and blue-black hair.
Friendships with Wally and Roy
worked much better
and getting out of
the shadow of the bat
was the best.
Nightwing—
your own man now.
I knew you could do it.

William Trowbridge

KONG LOOKS UP WHAT HE TAKES TO BE HIS NICKNAME

So, **monster**: "Any very large animal,
plant, or object." And more, after *adj*: "Gigantic,
huge, enormous," meaning that, when I'm next to
something small that utters words, each toe's
a monster, each eye, even my pointer, monstrous,
which explains this: "One who inspires horror
or disgust," likely why Fay so often
screams instead of talks, likely why
everybody does. Their smallness makes me
horrible. "Monster!" they shout and launch
the Dawn Patrol to pick me off, though
to the Latins, as distinct from the Dutch
and the Old French, the word means "Prodigy,"
which, in turn, to those same wise and no doubt
larger-than-usual people, means "Marvel."

Michael Arnzen

PROVERBS FOR MONSTERS

Slime never feels slimy to slime.
Bark all you like, the man in the moon has no ears.
Biting off the head silences the victim. But it is the feet that stop
them from running away.
Beware of things that go bump in the day.
Man, like monster, also has sharp teeth.
Those who most shun garlic, often most enjoyed it in their youth.
The sleep of madness brings forth humanity.
Wear gold jewelry. When silver is in fashion, wear even more of it.
Like a stake through the heart, so is the love of the clergy.
A man-eating plant will even swallow a vegetarian, when hungry.
A garbled threat is but a spell cast by an illiterate witch.
An infant vampire bites hardest.
Even werewolves shave during the day.
It is not your tentacles, but the acid that drips from them,
       that frightens your prey.
Those who fear the sun too soon often awaken before sundown.
One can catch a good human with a bad hamburger.
Holy water stings but a neck bite is forever.
Nothing is more stupid than an exposed brain.
Fortune favors the cleaver.

Curtis Scott Shumaker

GALACTUS: A DIPTYCH

I. Time

I am hunger unbounded.
I am the dragon Typhon,
the serpent Apophis,
swallowing light.
I devour the trees and rivers,
the rose growing by the riverside,
its subtle scent.
When I consume you,
it is more than your body
I erase, but all memory of you.
all you have built,
all you have unmade,
the effects of all your virtues
and all your crimes.
All the memories
of your existence.

That which I touch
I erase.
The great nations and their palaces,
the temples and their gods,
the seas and mountains
of planets and their moons.
Even the stars and the darkness between.
Cause and effect, desires and actions.
I will digest the universe.
My hunger is all that will remain.

II. Eternity

I am stillness, filled with vitality.
I am a river whose course does not change.
Through me, all waters flow.
I do not act, yet all action resides in me.
I fold all things into a single rubric.
I am a labyrinth in which all paths are tread at once.
A single, continuous note
which contains all harmony and melody.
One perfect number
which expresses all enumeration, every equation.
One source of light from which all color radiates
and returns to rest.
Those who rest in me
do not move, do not think,
yet experience all motion, all thoughts
as one.
Your indecision and anxiety,
The ignorance of your future, the longing for your past—
cast these aside
and rest in me.

Sarah Brown Weitzman

NOSFERATU THE VAMPYRE

There are none left now
to say what sort
of child he once was
or if he had been one

to sit too long indoors
a serious lad yet curious
about the rosy children
he watched from the tower.

Preferring fall's witherings
to spring's noisy beginnings
perhaps one winter day
he came upon a red berry bush

bent by the weight of ice.
Had he found that crush
of crimson upon the white neck
of snow wildly disturbing?

After that perhaps he couldn't stop
himself from attending the hunts
to the end, not quite knowing yet,
but nothing so crude

as beating the servants
or slicing away at the dogs.
What terrible thing
he eventually did

to become so corrupt
we'll never know.
Perhaps there was no intent
just a drift toward gore

and a failure to reflect
on what was happening to him.
In blind flight from feeling
yet craving others

perhaps he finally lit
upon a solution—
mistaking the sap
for the essence—

of drinking their blood.
Certainly his first taste
of women taken young
disappointed him. Doubly

penetrated they were not
one drop sweeter
than drained old men.
That once clean

fastidious boy now sleeps
on dirt, restless with dreams
of stakes and crosses
and sacred waters. Still he rises

to a kind of elegance
in transmuting to bat.
The metaphor's nearly religious:
blood of a savior

the flesh denied, a life
of ebony, crimson and moon silver.
So century after century
like a line of coffins following war,

he goes on surviving
when dying gives meaning to life,
a rich man living off others
yet resembling the rest

of us working men
despising his lot
despairing of any real change
or any way out.

Anne Bean

THE DECOMPOSITION OF ALEC HOLLAND

*We thought that the Swamp Thing was Alec Holland, somehow transformed
into a plant. It wasn't. It was a plant that thought it was Alec Holland...*
— Alan Moore, *Saga of the Swamp Thing*

You were buried without ceremony
in a back-acre of swamp:
the water your grave,
a mangrove tree your gravestone,
the duckweed your shroud.
No coins on the eyes, just silvery minnows.
No passage to the next world, just crawfish
snapping at your fingers and toes,
feeling what flesh would melt off your body
after three days in the wet.

When you came to that earthy, fetid place
you were made of bones and sinews,
muscles and bruises, vitreous humor,
hopes and hormones and regret.

As you rot, your body stops feeling, or
you stop feeling your body or
"body" and "feeling" become unbounded:
Too wet for chalk and anyway
your body's outline is no longer relevant.
The you-ness that is larger than your body
at last has space to grow properly,
to really put down roots.

Your bones are not bones;
now they are criss-crossing under the ground
a hundred miles in any direction.
Your flesh is not flesh,
it is water lilies and vines
and even the highest canopy of leaves
stretching up towards the sun.
Your worries are mosquitoes now;
your desires are crocodiles.

You are the soft rotting logs, the wading birds,
you are the stench of stagnant pools.

The boundaries that once defined you—
skin, hair, worry, regret—have gone now.
What remains is the weight of the water
What remains is the pull of gently insistent roots
What remains are the kudzu vines, creeping with ceaseless hunger.

William Trowbridge

THE MADNESS OF KONG

I think I see it now: they chase me
because I'm mad, and I'm mad because
they chase me. So said the doctor
when I told him I was kidnapped
from my secret island by movie men
and a tiny blonde in love with screaming,
that I was God and may still be,
that I'm immune to bombs and bullets.
He said it would be years before
I'm cured, that Mother is behind it all.
When I pinched his head, it made
a little squeak. Sometimes it's good
to be mad, if you really think about it.

Richard Newman

MOTHRA

Let's face it: I make a shitty monster. Moths
hardly instill fear in the hearts of man.
A cherry bomb could pound me back to powder,
and if the villagers only thought about it,
they could have simply built a giant bonfire
and I wouldn't have been able to resist—
I would have flown inside in a burning minute.

Did you know some moths have no mouths? They live
for seven days after sprouting wings,
time only to fuck, fly, and die.
Not me. I run at the mouth in my old age.
Now that my pupae have left the planet, I creep
down lonely streets at night, drawn to the few
windows not dark and shut but empty and blue.

Kurt Brown

THE HEAP

First of the muck-monsters stuck in a swamp,

Baron Von Emmelman, flying ace

from World War I bested in a dog fight,

face down in a mess of mud and algae

where his body simmered like a French fry

in a vat of oil. Though the Baron was dead

the life force in his cells was not, merging

with elements the swamp gave off—leafmold

and methane, scum and rot—for twenty years

until, heaved back by Nature's grim reluctance,

he rose again half man, half vegetable,

a mound of compost spoiling for a fight.

It's fear of evolution, of course, fear

that God's not God, Our-Father-Gowned-in-Light,

but a reeking sump of chemicals,

the Cesspool of the World. Once animate,

The Heap strode forth to battle Japs and Nazis,

propaganda's bully with viney arms,

brainless as a pumpkin but smart enough

to gobble common farm animals whole

because he couldn't breathe and needed fresh

oxygen from their blood. Despite such crass

table manners, The Heap was affable,

at least to boyish minds who'd never heard

of Darwin or his antique theories, fish

that crawled on land or winged dinosaurs.

But if they had, they would have understood,

knowing first-hand how all things finally rise

from sludge and gunk—pulsing , inchoate—

until the blood coheres, the brain swings wide,

and someone strides forth to conquer the world.

Evan J. Peterson

THE WUNDERKAMMER
(FRANKENSTEIN'S MONSTER TAKING INVENTORY)

My body museum, haunted by its own curiosities—
    a cabinet of wonders: tumescent chest,
    a cavity of breakthroughs, bursting;

this torso, cage of ribs, the bird inside grown wan
    since the clipping, stuffed now with batting,
    displayed like the Ashmole dodo,

the double heart clenching, bifid, a wounded
    gypsy moth pumping asymmetrical wings,
    the halves joined not by love but wire;

all of this, and yet no name;

that abdomen, distended by marvels, organs in pairs,
    trios, like the shared trunk of joined twins,
    straining the stitches to hold it all in;

three children's livers, pristine, unmarked by absinthe,
    unsoured by laudanum, three milk-fed
    miracles, drawing poisons from this well;

the extra pancreas, spleens, three kidneys,
    the small intestine shortened to make room
    and allow for quick excretion;

all of this, and yet no name;

this auxiliary breast, fat lurker beneath the pectoral,
    leathery nipple, hot as a witch's tit in a copper
    brazier, to suckle infernal familiars;

an extra lung, sponge for oxygen, drawing plenty,
    fuel for the flames at the core, goblin forge,
    a forest fire struck by one lucky bolt of light;

this skull inscribed, Hebrew scratched on the inside,
    illuminated by the flash: תמא , *Emet*, Truth,
    to crack open and rub off one glyph for Death;

all of this, and yet no name;

the brain in its cradle, swollen, backed up to the wall,
    the caul pinched together, cauterized, a barrier
    between tissue and fluid, envelope of genius;

whole corpus a jar of captured lightning, ultraviolet,
    the nerves like taut wires, humming
    seven feet from brain to heels—

here is my body, my *rarae aves*, my cartography.
    Here is called only Terra Incognita. Here
    be monsters.

Tony Barnstone

THE BLOWFLY THING

I heard a fly buzz when I died. I stepped
inside the chamber to be teleported,
and then it must have been a blue fly crept
inside with me, so when the atoms sorted
themselves again the circuitry gave off
a pop, a blue, uncertain, stumbling buzz.
I molted, left the corpse, and dug a trough
of earth. After a week, I rose, a fuzz
of beard below my chin, with great glass wings
and goggle eyes, a metal shell. I'm sorry.
I know I scare you, laying eggs in things
discarded (garbage, bodies) but don't worry,
blowflies like carnal angels with bug eyes
are born from death and kill death when they rise.

Kelly McQuain

VAMPIRELLA

It wasn't her boobs that appealed to this gay fellow
or the fact that she wore a red bikini thong.
She was a superhero with fangs, my gal Vampirella

—no tangled-up Rapunzel, no ashen Cinderella—
but an ass-kicker in knee boots ready to get it on
with any handsome, hot-blooded earthly fellow.

I fell under her spell too, I have to tell you,
though her curves didn't appeal to my ten-year-old dong.
Still I was bewitched and bedeviled by Vampirella

and her pulp-mag adventures, their pages long yellowed
along with old comics left in boxes too long.
In back of the Book Mart, past the fat owner fella,

is where I found her, a slick cover by Frazetta
peeking out past *Creepy* and *Eerie*, one shelf-rung
below forbidden *Playboy*: my wild bitch, *Vampirella!*

She fought werewolves, demons, witches, night terrors;
she seduced handsome men with her succubus song.
Though I followed her stories, I never could tell

a soul that I wanted what every straight fellow shouldn't:
to be a hot vampire chick and super-strong—
my high-heeled, raven-haired, bikini-clad Vampirella.

At ten, I was a good kid, no holy terror,
though I suspect my parents feared I was turning out wrong.
Maybe that's why they let their queer little fellow

spend his allowance on soft-core mags that might quell
a desire already starting to steer him along.
Blame me. Don't you dare blame double-D Vampirella.

Michael Arnzen

THE GENTLEST MONSTER

in the litter of writhing muck
the gentlest monster is the one
who obliges the others
by foregoing the prey mother
regurgitates into their beaks
on the hunt for human meat
he tarries behind and pretends
to be watching their backs
which is, actually, all he does
instead of studying their technique
while they flay their quarry fresh
in the cavernous dark lair of disgust
stripping the screamers of their skin
he tenderly prods his dinner with a claw
apologizing when he draws blood
the gentlest monster is the one
who starves and dies and resurrects
with a rage while they hibernate
murdering his beastie brothers
with the careful grinding of dull teeth

Ryan Bradley

OUR LOVE

Our love crashes down on skyscraping interracial taboos
Like Godzilla on Tokyo.

Our love climbs the tallest building in the city
And slaps down the planes of racism.

Our love flaps its enormous wings
And shoots laser breath at my grandmother.

Our love snatches my faults and throws them into a pod
While the locals question my strange behavior.

Our love, the misunderstood, maligned monster
Moves me.

Marge Simon

GODZILLA IN THERAPY

I'm single now.
I want sex all the time.
Sometimes I steal things,
little things.

They say it's a social phobia.
I open my mouth to roar,
but nothing happens.

Oh, the pain
of an obsessive-compulsive!
Always guess a cliché,
you won't be disappointed.

I see my face in multiples
in fifty-second floor windows
where humans hunch behind
walls of clean black glass.

There were four neurotics
in our group when we started.
I tried so hard to be good.

Our shrink is dead.
I hold the rest of us in my hand.
Ever so gently, I squeeze.

Now we are one.

Tony Barnstone

THE HUMAN TORCH

The spark of hunger, blast of lust, red flame
of the wet tongue. The heat of sex, rich flame
of the dark cunt, fire in the breath, stiff flame
of the white cock. These kindle the strange flames
of consciousness, his brain combusting, fire
of taste, ignited nose, his body's fire
like a deep smoldering house, his eye on fire
that sees the world consumed by clocks, slow fire
cremating us. Okay. So let him burn.
Let him be licked by tongues, go up a bonfire
of limbs, release the shot, the charge that fires
the gun. Burn clean, burn well. Let it all burn,
the savings, car, his love for one who's far
from loving back, the whole damn world on fire.

Chad Parmenter

Batman In Honey

—meaning love. Meet Julie Moneybunch,
     needy as a cathedral, oh yes, rose window

broken open, darkness in her narthex. She's nixed
     the waggle-dances of gangsters, been repaid

in spades by their noir icons: poison host,
     bap-bap-baptism by tommy gun. Second one

seeded her holy of holies with bullets. Holy
     Fertility, Batman, if the spent shells didn't evolve

to bumblebees, tumble free of the street
     to sting the hitmen. Julie wasn't even hurt. Ever

have such Hollywood miracles flowered here,
     on the pop top of hoodoo. Who wouldn't be

unsuited by her plea: Ditch the wings. Drink me
     honey. Especially remembering Joker's leggy cyborg,

the river of silver wire she cried on his eyes,
     her pelvic lasers set on Braise. Not much better,

that summer in Poison Ivy's winding thighs,
     green hands planting an itch deeper than feeling,

turning our hero to pillar of blisters. Lost lovers
     clutter his cave, molding shadows to hollow statues.

True, he's hottest for you, Gotham. Lines he writes,
     Christ—Rain is her hair. Neon a fringe in her lingerie

bridges. In your batblack alleys, he waits to cage
     the same dream that honeycombs puppy love—fantasy

as distance, drained of ways to render heroes drones.
     But his hive is night. He's already inside. So Julie

will stay sweet. Leave. Poor drone. This one will sting.

Jon Stone

*C*HAMBER

Some heroes smoulder, but not him,
whose heart's a bonfire that climbed upon him
and ate up his mouth.

He stands on the dam
a living flash fusion, bone to the upper jaw,
then cave-in, gulch of Venusian gas-storm.
Don't you know?

His lovesickness is volcanic.
His cry blows away houses.
The enemy of the world is bedazzled to a whimper.

Later, cooling in his own aftermath,
bandaged into a coma
and dreaming fitfully of hospitalised girlfriends,
he spits like spark welding,
a human Catherine Wheel.

Crystal Williams

"U're Looking More & More Like a Comic Book Hero"

Ty Avery O'Neill

Wolverine was cool, awesome
in a rugged sorta way. His hair, jet black
embers, danced a nasty funk two step,
& had moon-glow slitted eyes & a snarl
so sinister my thighs are still wobblin—
& wet & sweet. Wolverine was like *that*.

Had I been able I'da licked u offa them pages.
I'da swiveled my hips, tasted my lips,
murmured, *um um um. Damned.*
Can't keep from seein the pierce blue slash of u'r eyes,
from wondering at the funk in u'r hair, white
boy. Wanna cross these boundaries, drag my
palms on u'r skin, stick my fingers in u'r mouth & see
what'll become of 'em.

Raymond McDaniel

COLOSSAL BOY LOVES SHRINKING VIOLET

30th century and girls still hum, inarticulate,
to six-strings
in dorm rooms. She's deep as a well,
Imskian, shy there
on the sphere that dwindles like a candle.
His name is Gim-with-a-G Allon because
it's the future
and he fell into a comet's tail, or his spacecraft did,
and that's his origin,
much like that of Thom-with-an-H
Kallor, whose parents'
observation satellite was subject to another celestial trail.
Thom can induce
gravity's pull and increase the mass of objects and Gim
can get real real big.
He's always loved her but even more since she changed
to the new costume
with the black leather thigh-high fold-over boots.
She's a shrinker,
Salu Digby is: irised, down to a hair's width and clinging
to the lip
of her water glass during Legion roll-call.
And then one day
she slips into something more comfortable.
No one told
Duplicate Boy, of course, and then there was a fight,
and Boys Duplicate and Colossus
tore hell out of the Alps, though you would think Duplicate Boy
would have seen it coming,
what with a name
like Duplicate Boy, and who knows what he saw
with his duplicated X-ray vision,
even if he saw it
from planets away.

Maybe he saw his girl shrink to the size of a mite and dance
in the big man's
inner ear
until the hammer there tripped him dizzy, maybe she swam
up his caudate nucleus
and tricked its tunnel
with her green green fingernails.
Gim says he's always loved her but Phantom Girl,
that blabbermouth,
wants to know why he would take her somewhere as tacky
as the Alps
for their honeymoon. Meanwhile, Star Boy is wearing this new outfit,
a starfield?
His costume, it's made of stars.

Jason McCall

WHY THE SENTRY DOESN'T WRITE LOVE POEMS

My world goes dark every time you blink,
every time you see me and the silhouette
of other men. Am I just another gladiator
in this arena of champions and usurpers?
Can you see me through the cloak
and shield, the alliterate alias?

Where are you going?

More mother than mate, you're nervous whenever I play
god. I can move the universe and make it home
before dinner. What's the problem? My hands
could crush an atom, but they rest
on your hip; the mouth on your navel could swallow
a million suns. Doesn't that say it all?

Where do you go?

I never wanted hope on my shoulders,
never wanted to hear your heart
quicken by twelve percent every time I open the door.
I'd rather save us than the world. Remember, I didn't
fall from heaven. But if you leave, heaven,
every heaven, will fall.

David C. Kopaska-Merkel

Amazon Women and the Avocado of Doom

In the comic book, they had impossibly long legs,
very large antigravitational breasts (one each),
and eyes as big as their breasts should have been.
Young boys turned past pages advertising
inexpensive microscopes and books that explained
how to date girls, looking for more panels featuring
callipygian Greeks.

In reality, they hurried over the bumpy
olive-green surface, darting quick glances
over their muscular shoulders. The terrain was slippery
where there were bad spots in the fruit. They had to steady
themselves with their hands, but didn't fall, and kept arrows
at the ready.

In the comic book, they got into the sort of trouble
from which only a handsome man could extricate them.
Inexplicably, the most beautiful of the Amazons
would fall for their dashing savior. In the next issue
she was single once more and ready to be rescued
all over again.

In reality, there were no rescuers, and they had to do
all the saving for themselves. In the summer,
it was 100° in the shade, and there was no shade.
The avocado got pretty ripe, I can tell you, along
about mid-July.

In the comic book, trees grew and flocks of goats roamed
on the golf-turf-like surface of the giant fruit.
A handsome man wearing tight spandex
in bold colors and possessing peculiar powers
flew in from another comic book to save the day...
Again.

In reality, the weather in August was unseasonably hot
and the flesh of the fruit darkened and softened.
In the comic book, they all lived to fight another day
(remember that it was all written for small boys).

They sank beneath the surface, thrashing in futility,
mud flowing into their open mouths,
choking soundless screams.

They slogged through hip-deep mud and
barely made it to a waiting Blackhawk helicopter.
piloted by Captain America's good-looking brother.

Will Wells

BLUTO'S PLEA TO OLIVE OYL

You really need to dump the jerk—
that psycho who stuffs spinach in his pipe.
Talk about dangers of second-hand smoke!
The moron brags about "MUSKULS."
His largest squats between his ears,
his smallest one between his legs.
He sucks down cans of leafy Red Bull
like a human sinkhole.
But that doesn't explain his mood swings,
sudden rages, shrunken testes
and those male breasts he flexes
up and down like pistons while steam
blares factory whistles from his ears.
It's only a matter of time
till he buys an assault rifle
and wipes out Gold's Gym.

And you, my shiny one, sizzling
in the pan of my imagination,
my recipe for a healthy heart,
your one spit curl like the hand of God
extended in the Sistine Chapel.
You are the real eye-popper!
Come live with me, and be my condiment, O!
And I will be your red pimento.

Ron Koertge

KRYPTONITE

Lois liked to see the bullets bounce
off Superman's chest, and of course
she was proud when he leaned into
a locomotive and saved the crippled
orphan who had fallen on the tracks.

Yet on those long nights when he was
readjusting longitude or destroying
a meteor headed right for some nun,
Lois considered carrying just a smidgen
of kryptonite in her purse or at least
making a tincture to dab behind her ears.

She pictured his knees giving way,
the color draining from his cheeks.
He'd lie on the couch like a guy with
the flu, too weak to paint the front
porch or take out the garbage. She
could peek down his tights or draw
on his chest with a ball point. She
might even muss his hair and slap
him around.

"Hey, what'd I do?" he'd croak
just like a regular boyfriend. At last.

A. Van Jordan

THE UNCERTAINTY OF THE ATOM

DC Comics, February-March 1964, #11
"Voyage to Beyond!"

When I move, I deceive
the eye of anyone looking,

shining the light on what
they approximate as truth in their eyes.

If I turn the dial on my belt,
I can shrink to the size of a particle

of light. I can pass
through a crack in a wall at a speed

specified, but who knows where I'll land,
once on the other side. Life

for me is a battle against villains
and self; I never know

how the day will be inked,
how the story will twist.

I might foil the plans of a foe
one day, and, later that night,

find him lurking over my shoulder,
a new episode. When a seed

is blown in the wind, you never
predict the landing, a rock

or a pasture could be in the plan.
Some days, I'm caught in the hands

of enemies and something as
common as turning on a light

while walking into a room, can change
the course of a day. I'll escape, maybe

weigh the villain down like a full-grown man
for a necktie or make myself

infinitesimal, less than a mosquito's proboscis,
which she only reveals, moments later,

by the bump on your thigh.
Or, in a breeze, I'll float like a leaf

you brush from your hair.
My life finds me with you whom I love

and you who will never love me;
of how you'll greet me, I'm never certain:

one minute I'm nowhere and the next,
sun streams through a crack in an open door,

and you cannot bear the weight of what you see.

V Santiesteban

STORM, FROM THE CAGE

I've spread my legs for bonds greater than these,
taken homes amongst oceans and bedlam trees
whose branches shake with every gale until
the sweetest fruits fall at my feet like hail.

Hurricanes assemble beneath my feet. Their eyes
take my hands and lead me to lands where winds
of different names kiss until passion turns
ripe with fury and is blessed.

I've lost nothing a black cloud won't yield
and for the gods in me I have never nailed hope
to any ground. Land's rich, profound gestures
tease my senses in vain. I tongue-kiss tornadoes

and come like rain. Restraint is a story for sleep.
I'll cry in your arms and pity the feet you plant
for one season then let spoil the next with your dull,
devoted neglect. I've spread my legs for bonds

greater than these. I've emptied my pockets of soil
and leaves. I've packed boxes of lightening addressed
but not yet sent and have only this once felt a tinge
of regret. In your arms clear skies build for a time

then part in soft breezes, pacific and kind. But you are
no tempest, your world is too calm, when we shape
for love, there's no wind in your song. Don't make me
do it my way. You've the key. Now let me. Let me.

John Rodriguez

THE HEART MISSES WHAT THE EYE CAN'T SEE

Very few people know this,
how everything I see is red.
My friends are nothing
more than crimson-hued
silhouettes, some flat and liquid like
blood, warm expanding pulses
for others. You were electric
rose simmer from your center
of gravity outwards, a vessel ablaze
—no one else looks like that.
That's what I loved about you first,
then you chose me. All of us
thought it would be Warren,
rich, handsome, and distant—as if
the wings were not enough—
instead you chose the team's true beast.
(Don't argue, Jean. I can still hear you,

remember?) Think of it like this:
everything I see shatters,
more so than any other man,
which means the woman I love
I must never see. This is why
I loved you, Jean, when everything
you touched you burned. I loved you
when your essence refused to be
mortal. I like to think we found
the cosmos within each other, a power
to outshine suns. We were Phoenix and Cyclops
in love, some say Orpheus and Eurydice
for a new era. I would go to hell
and back for you, but I would fail
for the same reason. Knowing you
are with me isn't enough,
if I can't see your face and not lose you.

Marion Shore

Bizarro World

Remember Bizarro World, in Superman?
that square-shaped planet somewhere out in space
(hatched from one of Lex Luthor's wackier plans),
home to Bizarros, pale and cracked of face,
each one an imitation, flawed and weak,
of Superman himself, or Lois Lane—
inarticulate beings, who only speak
in opposites—which somehow might explain
why the world has lately seemed flat-sided,
and why our love has felt to you and me
like a poor clone of itself (though we've denied it).
Is this Bizarro world? And might we be
only a pallid copy of the two
of us: Bizarro me, Bizarro you?

Lara Eckener

ROOF SLIP NOIR

Babel tells him she loves him.
He listens, unbelieving,
thinks she's forgotten
how to do anything else.
She doesn't reach into the darkness for him
anymore.

She expects him to come to her ready,
lies open to him in the pale orange glow of her streetlights
and inhales, waiting to be the thing he needs.
He does little more than mark her.
The trails of his fingers leave streaks in the dust
across her face.
He hopes to one day rub the sweat into her eyes.
In the dark, unseeing, she'll remember him
as the boy swinging from her fire escapes,
practicing, eager to begin.

He works easily within her,
taking advantage of her distraction.
On slow nights he leaves his guns at home,
paces her borders,
looking to see if they've slipped.
He's so busy feeling benevolent for not leaving her
that he forgets she can roll up her sidewalks
and leave him out on his own.
He trusts that he could lose himself to her.
It would be easier than reinventing himself
every night.

Each new barrier she erects
is a wider, darker memory than the last
for him to avenge.
The maps of the well-worn pathways of his patrols
all belong to salesman.
They claim to be able to unmask him.

They will tell you where he is
for a price.
Because a city without a hero
will stand silent.
All they want is rest.

A hero without a city is aimless.
Afraid the echoing ricochet of his wild fire
might kill him.
A city without a hero is just a city.
In fear, Babel tells him
she loves him.
He brushes it off,
puts on his mask.

Bryan D. Dietrich

SUPERMAN'S *OTHER* SECRET

Alis Volat Propriis

It's strange, I suppose, to find myself spellbound,
in knots, as tongue-tied by her tossed locks
as the proverbial bad boy. Lassoed, trussed up
and forced to tell the truth under the influence
of that golden rope, doped. Lost in her main
means of defense, more shackled than she
by her mettle, those magic manacles. Unable
to dodge the bullets that, heartward, seem to hum.
Mostly, she avoids them. I just let them come.

I'm supposed to be taken, I know. Good guy,
steady as the morning star, faithful as that apple
pie Lois sometimes bakes me, a *fine* example….
But then there's two of me, as many (more?) of her.
Smart, savvy, strong enough to beat all she can't
bear. As beautiful as any stag she might have done
in, outrun, caught, antlers askance, standing
in the still. Goddess? Okay, demi-, but born to shame
that lack of choice, Paradise, from which she sprang.

Woman of steel, mistress of the upper air,
she knows how each of us is always already
falling. Alone with her, I seem to understand
earth, its breath, better, the orgasm of ozone
that rushes out when she describes her own
flight. Even sitting—stratus, nimbostratus,
talking—I've watched her turn into it, dive,
ride it the way she does her stories, worries, cares.
The shape of the wind. What her world wears.

Me, I just point and leap, but not with her.
Some days I fear that I'm invisible as the plane
she doesn't need, a spectacle in a suit, uptight,
upright, perhaps *too*. Or that, though our colors clash

the same, hers cut closer to the breast. Even weaknesses….
I fear mine are mine alone. No recurring villains,
no green rocks, a decided lack of chains. And though
we both could leap this difference, in fact much less,
there is a yaw yet, deep as regret, from farmboy to finesse.

Jason Schossler

TONGUE-TIED

Don't fall for me, farm boy. I don't have time for you.
—Lois Lane to Clark Kent, *Lois & Clark*

She'd be sitting in the desk four rows
in front of mine, little strands
of blond hair hanging loose
from her ponytail,
when the tidal wave struck
Saint Joseph's Catholic School,
plaster crumbling, aisles flooding,
and me without a phone booth,
forced to slip into my red boots and trunks
under cover of the pull-down
Bible Lands map. After shouldering
the weight of thousands of tons
of falling brick, I'd freeze
the water into an iceberg
with a blast of my super-breath,
and then fly my classmates to higher ground,
starting with that girl whose desk
I passed without ever asking for pen
or paper or Saturday matinee,
her fingers cupping my shoulders
as I set her safely down
in Point Park, still breathing in my cape,
wanting to know who I was, and where
I was from, and not a peep out of me
as I swooped back into the sky,
the need for words having been
forever washed away.

Lisa Cheby

Love Lesson #24 from Buffy the Vampire Slayer

all this world's an open

                grave
                    as love is
                        open

for fallage in by
      my unchosen one:
                    I am God's promise,

but what of your promise of love?
                      We toil against gravity
                        all day.

            I do not want to wait
            to fall
            in line.
            I claw
out of the gravity
of your promise

        and engrave my own
      in earth: do not surrender

to gravity:
           though you lie   open
                        as a grave

          sooner or later
          that excuse
               just stops working

               promises Xander
               descended from the Greek
               to defend men

who have not fallen in
                    place: alias: love
                                        is my gravity

keeps me gravely moving graveward
to the hellmouthy gravity of my unreality

(and by grave I mean you)

(and by unreality I mean :

I am the open one
waiting for someone
unwilling to fall).

Joe Castle

CLARK

I tread a fresh garden
of cirrus and nacreous
and listen to the clamour
of weevils and aphids

whose armour grates
with static skitter
among the ears of wheat
that wait for day.

The dying night
unfurls a wet haze
to hide her from me—
I take a breath and brew

a hurricane
inside my chest
to strip the morning
of her damp chiffon.

She slips into my pores
and stands up my hair
like the golden fields
down below me,

cut now to chaff
by the combine snarl
of Pa's old Gleaner—
our rusty rhino beetle.

A flush fills my face
with hot and numb,
searing my eyes
to molten rubies.

I hear my father wave
and with a glance
I mute the land
to cloud and ash.

Albert Wendland

What the Joker Said to Batman

Oh, my sweet dear—together again!
Here alone at the end of the world
To fill our part as prime entertainment,
Ultimate symbol for the clotted masses—
Objective correlative, repression made flesh,
Postmodern anti-human sustenance for zombies,
For the media-sterilized who *need* our extremes.
As the world dies, you and I, my love,
Will live on . . . in pain.

Obsession versus madness, avenger versus clown—
Operatic violence for a world that sinks
In wide decay and endless apocalypse.
Oh, we *are* the future!
When all's unreal, and the unreal is bland,
We'll thrive, endeavor, in perfect adaptation,
We'll waltz, consume, love, hate,
And justify each other's reason to live—
Exist for the sins of the plugged-in, turned-on,
Tuned-out weaklings, self-made failures
Lost in their out-of-control creation,
Drowning in reified digitized truth—
They *need* our pain to know they're alive.
If they are.
But who cares, Batman? We're what matters.
We've torn ourselves away from mediocrity, history.
No one dares reify us.
We're clear, pristine, in *perfect* combat.

So come on, dark angel.
Wrestle with your green-white demon once more,
Beat me till wine-colored streams cross
My bone-white skin in branches of blood.
I'll slaughter your loved ones. You'll hate me hard.
When others can't sing from boredom and pallor
We'll provide them song—intensified, mythologized!

So get it up, Batman—
They've paid with their lives,
With all they ever wanted
Out of futures and pasts.
We'll give them their ultimate
And *only* expiation.
Let's be good. Commence!
And bite me—
Dark lover.

Greg Santos

HULK SMASH!

I am the least difficult of men. All I want is boundless love.
—Frank O'Hara, "Meditations in an Emergency"

Hulk know. Hulk have problem.
Hulk took break from Avengers after orphanage and tanker truck incident.
Hulk's therapist said it cry for help.
Hulk said, "Hulk strong! Hulk self-reliant! Ugh!"
Who Hulk kidding? Hulk not really so incredible.
Hulk look in mirror everyday and want to smash things.
Hulk never cut out to be superhero.
Hulk really just regular Joe.
Hulk got Hungry Hungry Hippos for birthday.
But no one want to play with Hulk. Everyone too busy saving world.
Hulk like watching Tennessee Titans with bowl of chips and dip.
Hulk like to go beachcombing for giant squid carcasses.
Hulk OK guy. Just misunderstood.
Hulk really just want to have normal 9 to 5 job.
But who will hire Hulk?
Hulk first tried 7-11 cashier job in Schertz, Texas.
Hulk wore stupid uniform even though it too small.
Hulk want to smash Slurpee machine.
Hulk think it give too much ice, not enough syrup!
Captain America lecture Hulk. Captain America douchebag.
Hulk tried work in office job.
Hulk carpool with Joan and Frank from accounting.
Hulk wear snappy tie and dress shirt.
Hulk even bought new purple pants!
Cubicles too small for Hulk.
Hulk hate paperwork!
Hulk smash paper shredder!
Hulk get yelled at by Shelley in adjacent cubicle.
Hulk hate Shelley! (Hulk think about Shelley every day.)

John Rodriguez

PHOENIX, INTERRUPTED

Because the publisher felt I should die for my sins.
Because I murdered five billion people.
Because I swallowed a sun.
Because I could.
Because of the Phoenix Force.
Because it will take Susan Richards 24 years to go from being
        the Invisible Girl to the Invisible Woman.
Because of Wonder Woman.
Because of Nightcrawler, Colossus, Storm, Banshee, Thunderbird, and
        Wolverine.
Because of a writer named Chris Claremont.
Because of low sales.
Because force fields and lasers were no longer enough.
Because of an artist named Jack Kirby.
Because Beast, Angel, and Iceman needed more of the panel.
Because you and I were the second rank, Scott.
Because red-blooded American boys need leaders and redheads
        in short dresses.
Because comic books are for boys.
Because a Brooklyn boy named Stan Lee wanted a team of teenage heroes
        each with a power of Superman's.
Because I was invulnerable and you had the vision.
Because I needed to be wounded, but all you needed was a cause.

Gary Jackson

SUPERIA'S SWAN SONG

Unloaded six rounds into my temple, only to dye
a tuft of hair gunpowder gray. Paid the metallurgist
to take a chainsaw to my neck but the teeth cracked

against my throat. Jumped into a volcano just
to vomit silica. Sometimes ignorance is a dropped pen
on the sidewalk: an invitation to peer through concrete
cracks, spy the center of the earth—a globe of light.

It would take so little to reach, to rip it from its moorings,
split us open. And how that thought gave birth to others—
all the beautiful ways to yoke us to oblivion. You cling

to faith like yellow to newspapers while I struggle
to reach the sun, yet keep falling back to orbit. All
of us victims of our own truths, brutal and heavenly.

V Santiesteban

KITTY PRYDE CONSIDERS DROWNING

I know how dramatic that title sounds
but I've no control over

the writers and the writers are gulls.
Illustrators as well. I've this one

opportunity to tell the truth since
we're phasing somewhere in the middle

of nowhere right now, me: Pryde—you:
reader—so listen: my Savta Prydeman

balanced six days on a tiny metal plinth
in a sunken Nazi cell before she finally

fell. The first time she spoke to me
in a dream she confessed, "Cruelty

is fathomless, drowning painless."
Her voice was soft as wet paper tearing.

When I confided her visit to my saba
he looked at me as if I were a monster.

"There is only one peace," he screamed,
"and that is the infinite space between breaths."

I was only a child, neither cruel nor immune,
and my saba's rage schooled me.

Fortitude, tenacity, hubris, nothing will save you
when the dark clerks claim your kind.

We are all exactly alike, my fellow monsters,
my friends. Weeks without bread. Days without

water. Minutes without air. Now, inhale
to return. Exhale and you can't come back.

Joey Nicoletti

THE DEATH OF CAPTAIN MARVEL

after the graphic novel by Jim Starlin

When Captain Marvel died,

the stars became

splotches of detergent.

When Captain Marvel died

of cancer, my candy-cigarette days

smoldered in my father's ashtray.

When Captain Marvel died,

my uncle's tour bus stalled on bridges

gripped in frost and soot.

I was a cracked fire hydrant,

calling out my big sister's name

in my watery dialect.

I was a pair of boots, an olive-green and yellow

pair of rubber boots who slipped

on a sidewalk being fitted

in a new see-through dress of ice.

I was a soccer ball

with a small hole, losing air slowly,

like my mother was

in her hospital room.

When Captain Marvel, the most

cosmic superhero of all died,

he was surrounded by family and friends,

like my mother was
in her final days. A few pages

before Captain Marvel died,

Spider-Man abruptly walked out

of the Captain's chambers, overcome

by shock and disbelief. I saw my face

beneath his mask: blood-shot

eyes dilated with the awful fear of death;

his head looking backwards, like mine

in Mount Sinai Hospital;

breathless, defenseless, no web to spin,

only sweaty palms:

one to place on my sister's shoulder,

the other to rub my eyes

after we said our good-byes;

my sister and I walking down a hallway

of dim, sickly light.

Lesley Wheeler

EARTH-TWO SONNET

A caped figure slips through an empty building, inked figment on the brink
of the place where General Lee, tired of fighting, swore to serve as president.
Books wait breathless in their boxes; renovation's imminent.
The blackboards ache like thunderclouds. Power trying to break.

At dinner, it's all doppelgangers and secret identities. *Captain America's
	shield is the Marvel standard for durability,*
he explains as our son lists mythic forces that might shatter its
flawlessness. Nova Heat from the Human Torch; Hulk's avocado fist.
Their mirror-faces glow. *Maybe Thor's hammer,* they agree.

May that hammer slam
this Earth-One heroine. Let her drop the shield, ride the bolt to a parallel
	dimension and learn
to be ordinary. Let the afternoon level its cosmic rays at my back, burn
the scar-shadow-stain of the last few years onto the linoleum,

sketching a record of the armor I recycle, the tights I now peel free.
Allowed to wrinkle; skip a meeting of the League; be indiscreet. Her
	perfection only legend now. Vibranium chip of history.

Katerina Stoykova-Klemer

THE SUPERHERO IS MOVING OUT

In his wife's smallest suitcase
he packs:
> a toothbrush
> a change of tights.

In a long row
with boogers and tears smeared
across their cheeks,
his children stare at him.

As he approaches the door,
the stove timer goes off.

*Would you like to have dinner
with us?* His aproned wife
emerges from the kitchen.

For one last time, he sits
at the head of the table, his back
to the large windows with
sinister city lights.

She serves potatoes
and lamb. His favorite.

They eat in silence, while
the dishwasher hurls
water from side to side.

*Do you want me to drive you
to the airport?* she asks.
No, thank you, he answers. *I'll fly.*

Ann Cefola

How My Father Looked Like Superman

The round face, square head—
thick hair weighted by Vitalis
and off-center part.
The horned-rimmed glasses,
a trompe-l'oeil wood frame to the eyes.
Tall, no cape
but a navy blue uniform,
white gloves, a badge—
on Sundays so suburban worshippers
could arrive, depart without mishap.
This invisible service,
far from Metropolis
where he traveled through space,
selling it for advertisers.

Like that TV Superman,
he leapt off a building.
I watched him fall
for 33 years,
a slow-motion stunt.
My mother collapsed trying
to out-chase that descent,
my brother with a megaphone,
coaching flight technique,
and me, behind a sealed window,
sinking into gravity.

When we found him,
the air had reshaped him,
his hair as white as Jor-el's,
and skin orange as Mars.
I pulled from my purse a curled snapshot—
hand at attention and lips, a smile.
Could that picture breathe life into him again?
Instead, a tear drops like a final sigh:
Clark Kent finding Superman
unable to fly.

Eric Morago

THOR LOSES HIS HAMMER

He staggers into my home tear-drunk
gold locks reeking of booze and puke,
snot dangling from his perfect nose.
I ask, *What happened?*

It's gone, he says, *I can't find it.*

He sits, sinks into the cushions,
cries more than any god should.
Loki? I suggest, quick to help.

First place I tried—beat him to a pulp
then ransacked the underworld.
Hela told me to check with the frost giants.
No luck there, either.

As he speaks his voice shakes
with so much loss I ache for him—
helplessly, like having to see a child
break, bawling over a popped balloon.

I brew us coffee.
He takes the mug in his large god hands,
thanks me and asks what he should do.

Can't the dwarves just make another?

He says I don't understand.
Tells me it was a gift from Odin—
the only hard proof of his father's love.

But I do—years before my father left,
he gave me a watch I'd never wear,
but made promise to always keep.
Now it rests in a sleek black box,
tucked away in my bedside drawer.

Often I forget it's there, except
on nights I can't sleep, when I hear
its faint ticking, and think to take it
from its grave, to feel the weight
of my father's heart in my palm.

I want to tell Thor I understand,
but he has passed out on my couch,
curled into a muscular ball, snoring—
and I wonder,

if Thor cannot find his hammer,
how long before we all feel his loss,
how long before we miss the thunder
from our skies.

Amanda Chiado

FLOATING IN JÄGERMEISTER

Batman chomps heads off bats
like Ozzy when he gets blasted.
Up-heaves a memory-grave, his father
flung like yesterday's newspaper.

Clumps of muddy-blood stuck
in the rabbit fur his mother wore
that night at the opera. A plane drifts
feather dust before it's smithereens.

Batman's brain whirls like cotton candy.
How does it feel to be a dead man
not just float like one?

When Batman gets smashed
he puckers up to women
who are 5's and 3's, spreads
his buttery eroticism of wings.

He starts to whip with pleasure
if one knocks her head back
rolling her eyes, her legs
flightless birds, except in bed.

Batman remembers being new,
a knot of veins, plucked from a cave.
He wishes he might resurrect time,
but that just makes him drink more.

And the shot glass hollers.
Let's dive and die again
cling to ceilings instead of
grounds stuffed with the dead.

Batman touches his body
like a blind man, echolocation.
Booze and a night suit: an embrace
without a person to complicate it.

George Longenecker

SUPERBOY

Gray twilight between past and present,
the scent of old oak drawers with
Superboy comics, *MAD Magazines*,
marbles and three-cent Liberty stamps.

I climbed the sugar maple in the backyard,
walked the Boston and Maine Railroad tracks,
scaled the town water tower,
awoke to robin's songs on summer mornings.

I was Superboy looking for new places to fly,
Superboy who could lift trains from their tracks,
who could alight on the water tower and watch the town below,
who could swoop down to rescue my grandmother—
Superboy disguised as an ordinary schoolboy
mowing the lawn and weeding the iris beds.

Superboy rides his bicycle on the paper route
delivering the afternoon *Globe* and *Traveler*—
ducks into his grandmother's cellar
and emerges immortal and indestructible,
defying gravity and leaping above the lampposts,
so high over town he can see the ocean.

On a branch halfway up the sugar maple,
he's hidden by leaves, so nobody knows
he's disappeared into a *Superboy* comic book.
He swoops out of the leaves, cape trailing,
a streak in the sky flying into the sun—
indestructible and immortal—
powerless to find truth, justice and the American way,
powerless to find
himself.
Superboy

Michael Schmeltzer

MAN OF STEEL, MISHEARD

Because the nurse slurs
the words together, *Man of*

becomes *Manna*—a meal
from heaven. Is that why

the child chews through
Superman comics

as if every issue
was a sheet of jerky?

He needs to steel
the body against solitude,

against a fortress
hijacked by sickness.

He gazes out the window
for rescue. No heroes, just icicles

hanging by their fingertips,
the skim milk of moonlight

spilling on burnt toast.
The morning his heart stopped

then restarted
remains the crumbling building

the family can't leap over.
Some days they read to him.

Other days they tell him jokes
that bounce off his chest like bullets.

Whichever one of them laughs
is the criminal holding the gun.

Marta Ferguson

ORACLE TRASHES THE CHAIR

> *Let's get this out of the way first. There is absolutely no reason why Barbara*
> *Gordon should be in a wheelchair.*
> —Ray Tate, *Comics Bulletin*

Well, not *no reason*.
I'm not saying I'm excited
to be here. That I'd rather
pop wheelies and glory in
my upper body strength
than be the lithe-limbed girl
I was before the bullet.

But then I hadn't been a girl
for years, had I? Senator,
woman of a certain age,
whose goodness must somehow
be suspect. *Not true!* They cry—
we've achieved equal rights
here in the comics sphere—
and yet. Is that what Selina'd say?
Or Ivy?

The choice is this—good girl
or villainess and no one wanted
to see Batgirl go bad. So here I am.
Unsexed. A neuter in the chair
whose intellect rolls unfettered
in the cause of good.

I make the tough calls just like the boys,
let my girls fly with wings
I have not found.

Cathryn Cofell

AQUAMAN, BEACHED

I am in up to my belly.
Still as lime at the bottom
of a rented tub in a rented room
on the east side of Milwaukee.
Knees jammed against the backsplash,
hands like sea moss, head under,
blowing bubbles in this foul water.
Wondering what I did to sink so low.
Cancelled.
Replaced by a talking cow and chicken.
Some carp about ratings and demographics.
Now, I'm a sperm whale without a mate,
every black-book number dialed, black-balled.
Sure, the first dates come easy, my tight green
pants and matching boots and me,
eager to please. But inevitably, the gills.
The *Jesus-mary-and-joseph*
what in God's name is that?
And her flop off the couch and the-stumble-
like-hell and the-never-look-back.
Even Wonder Woman flew off
when all I could offer were coffin-tight lungs
and a weird way with fish.
No cape. No fancy belt. No escape,
even, in Lake Michigan since
that couple on the beach saw me
go in but not come out.
Now, I'm the wrong kind of news,
a coral reef waiting
for rerun syndication, turtleneck
weather, the new girl in town.

Ravi Shankar

FALSIFIABILITY

> *There was a smash. There was an explosion. There was foam and confusion. The imagination had dashed itself against something hard.* —Virginia Woolf

In post-Artemis posture, with red thigh-highs,
spangled bustier, lasso of truth and unbreakable

tiara, Wonder Woman was invented by Moulton
Marston *after* the systolic blood-pressure test,

progenitor to the polygraph. Catch a liar
by the tale, hooked by chest to convolute

rubber tubes, metal plates on fingers to record
the production of sweat glands. It's a mainstay

now of Forensic Assessment Interview Techniques,
or *FAINT*, admissible as evidence in federal court.

Forged from links snipped from the Golden
Girdle of Gaea, Wonder Woman's infinitely elastic

lasso can compel anyone in its orbit to speak
the truth, else to obey the will of the wielder.

"Under no possible condition," Marston wrote,
"can true submission be unpleasant." Giving in

is not verisimilitude, yet that which is scientific
by its very nature can be proven false. Take

the particles of light that beamed Lynda Carter
into my childhood family room, where I laid,

hips jammed into a throw pillow to watch her
twirl, glasses off, arms outstretched, to emerge

from a thunderclap of light, ready to fight Nazis.
Perhaps corpuscles emitted by luminous bodies,

perhaps waveform resounding in the ether,
else born of some admixture, each new theory

of light offers greater descriptive power
with even greater occasion for its own eventual

falsification, thus making it even truer.
According to released FBI files, Marston lied

about the effectiveness of lie detector tests
in order to shill for Gillette razors, measuring

subjects' involuntary reactions in ads finding
the brand's blades minimized the emotional

disturbances caused by competitors' products.
Because true smoothness never chafes or burns.

Marston lived polyamorously with two women,
attended clandestine sorority initiation rituals

where coeds would tie each other up. Research
that proved he found Jung's anima in himself,

a primordial, Amazonian, inborn nature
that needed to be lovingly bound and spanked

therapeutically. He was a woman who bore
the fib of masculinity, all the more male

for surrendering helplessly to her dictation.
Years after his death, Gloria Steinem would

splash Wonder Woman of the adamantine
bracelets, patriotic panties, and roundhouse

boot-kicks, founding member of the Justice
League, on the very first cover of *Ms. Magazine.*

A fantasy turned feminist-icon. "The truth
will set you free," Steinem said in speeches,

"but first, it will piss you off." Taken literally,
polygraph means many writings, not the law

of the father, but *l'écriture feminine* gravid
inside each mother tongue, a dark pool where

the largest fish slumber, a clitoral, uterine
text that resists both status quo & over-

determination. Like a lasso that reveals truth
to be no more than a closed system of Lies.

Adrian Matejka

"America's First and Foremost Black Superstar"

Gotta be a frame: Luke Cage, Hero for Hire stuck
in Texas. Me—luckier than any *seven* dudes
you know—left in a box, stashed in a jive-ass attic.
What's the beef, man? This ain't no shakedown,
but it smells like Seagate all over again: one cell
leads to another and the story don't never finish.
Who's hiring me in this box? Sure, them foxes
are here with me, but I never get at 'em unless
I'm bailing those broads out of one scrape or another.
And I still don't get no residuals. Christmas,
what's the point of being a hero for hire when you
give out more free shit than a schoolyard pusher?
I got bullet-proof skin and I'm meaner
than Jerome Mackey *and* Jim Kelly in a paper bag.
But what good is steel skin if it bounce
the same blades and boots all the time?
I'll give you five to one it ain't fun. Let Cage
get at some of that Texas barbeque. Let Cage bang
some Southern heads on the way. Christmas,
let Cage change his threads. I've been sporting
blue pants and a yellow shirt since '71. Forget
this chain-link for a belt or the metal wristbands.
Dig it, I just want to step out for a minute—
I hear those black power muthas calling stereotype.
But they don't say nothing about that voodoo mixing,
corn-rowed chump, the Witchdoctor. They don't say
nothing about my boy the Black Panther. Man,
those boys at Marvel even gave me a white sidekick:
Iron Fist. A white boy who knows kung fu, winging
a black man. Ain't that something?

Ross White

DR. MANHATTAN MEDITATES BEFORE DEPARTING FOR MARS

I am unaware of the glow sometimes, the faint blue and warm
radiance of my presence. I still think myself a static assembly
of proton, carbon, salt and phosphorus: flesh and bone. Man.
I can be that, looking on in wonder at an electron storm,
can be scientist Jon Osterman exploring a universal anomaly.
But in reflections, photos, the eyes of others? I am post-human.

The press has linked me to a cancer scare. My research
so preoccupies me that I sent a copy of myself to make love
to Laurie while continuing to work in my laboratory.
Perhaps I am dangerous. Perhaps I have lost touch.

But I have fought for my country, tried not to live above
the people I—when I was Osterman—loved dearly,
only to discover that every action and response is preordained.
Forty minutes from now, July 1986, it begins to rain.

Jarret Keene

CAPTAIN AMERICA AT HOME

for Jack Kirby

After a long day of cracking Red Skull's
skull, he is sofa-bound, polishing the star-
spangled shield that protects him from
the transforming powers of the Cosmic
Cube, the swarming gadgetry of Baron
Zemo, the deadly karate chops of the
Super-Adaptoids. For now, he is happy.
The TV is on, background noise he needs
to drown his fears and concentrate;
the gauntlets, literally, are off. Tonight
he will shine his shield, stitch his winged
mask, and catch a few sound bites on
Headline News. That's the plan.

But then the unthinkable occurs: he sees
that the white star of his jersey contains
a bloodstain in the shape of his country's
mainland, forty-eight states, all of which
he's saved more than once from mind-
control, mass murder, General Mayhem.
He ponders the magnitude of his job,
the awesome responsibility of defending
not only the land of freedom but also the
free world. It seems too much, really,
for one man alone. Which is how he feels
most of the time, isolated from the citizenry
he has sworn to protect. For a moment,

he ponders life without a country,
a nomadic existence, a self-imposed exile,
allowing his lungs to swell proudly,
like birthday balloons. To inhale *clean* air,
air minus the taint of patriotism, Puritanism,
"mobocracy." To talk with people as if
they were real, not just some glorified

abstraction. *But enough!* He shakes himself
like a wet dog, gets up to toss the soiled
jersey into the washer. Meanwhile, the bald
eagle statuette that squats atop his mantlepiece
squints fiercely and prepares for flight.

Jon Stone

DEAREST WOLVERINE,

come in. I'm sorry I haven't been in touch. It's just
the cake's all gone. They've had enough cut and thrust,
enough of your wipe-clean claws and wired-fierce skull
bemusing their shelves. But even the most truculent covergirl
sees her star fail eventually, no matter how much steak
she makes of the goon squad. There's no single ringing mistake,
just the horizon beyond which your jokes creak like crickets,
where even those most taken with your wrenched tourniquets,
your intimate sufferings, see now a skin as thick as a Panzer's
and meshed with rabbit snares, unpick the bloated Windsor
studding the neck of your myth and watch its head roll forward
like a fumbled bauble. I'm sorry. I guess they got tired
of every ugly thing you threaten scuttling into a shadow-soup
deep and dark as the skeins of blood you unloop and unloop,
every one a padlock to your fists' sprung skeleton keys.
I guess your name is the sound of gum being chewed in their ears
and they wonder why no beast of a wind or wind-shagged beast
is ever allowed to muss your horned hair, I guess. I guess at least
some of them are reminded of someone who bruised them.
I guess the world is full enough of powerful, lonely men.

Stephen Burt

SELF-PORTRAIT AS KITTY PRYDE

I have been identified
as gifted & dangerous. People fight over me
but not in the ways I want. Who would expect
it in a girl from Deerfield, Illinois,
town of strict zoning, no neon & quality schools?
I pass through difficult physical laws, cement,
flames, cupboards, crowds, tree trunks & arguments,
precociously, like something to protect.
I am always going through some phase.

My best friend spent apprentice years
alone inside a study like a star.
My wide eyes & Jewish hair
are shyness, a challenge to artists, &
untouchable. I can slip out of the back of a car.
When I am tired I dance, or pace
barefoot on the civilian ground
of Salem Center, where rain falls through me.
I have begun to learn to walk on air.

Adventures overemphasize my age.
In my distant & plausible future I will bear
one child, scorn, twenty-five pounds
of technology on my back, & the further weight
of giving orders to a restless band
of misfits who save America from its own rage
but cannot save themselves, & stay up late.
My friends & the fate of the world will have come to rest,
unexpected, staccato, in my sophomore hands.

Krista Franklin

STORM RETHINKS HER POSITION

At my vanity, I brush the stars
from my hair, listen
to the bones of my friends
as they settle into their chambers.
One cough, wet as the clouds
I gather around me like children,
lands muffled on my ears.

Outside, Wolverine's bike roars to life, shrinks
to a small buzz swallowed in the distance.
(He roams until dawn, pacing
his pocked memory, lying in the hollows
hoping the darkness offers a clue of who he is.)
While the bristles move through, I nervously mull
over Magneto's proposition, praying
the Professor has closed his mind for the evening,
that Cerebro has sighed herself to sleep.

There is sense in Magneto's position; this madman
whose body is a nest of the electromagnetic,
who makes a home for us higher than I've ever flown—
where Venus slowly rotates like a woman
appraising herself in her mirror.
All my life on this planet spent in service
of others, the elements that converge in my breast
for their protection bow to me like the small humans
in the village of my mother when I was a girl, a waterfall
spray of albino cornrows washing down my shoulders.

I try to remember a moment of humanity, a memory
not contaminated with their hatred
(the kaleidoscope of genocide they spin before our eyes).
I think of the vow I have made, the laughter of my family,
their magic crackling in the air around me,
and wonder what freedom tastes like.

Lynette DiPalma

WHEN SUPERMAN DREAMS

When Superman dreams, the city
is quiet. He does not fly, but takes
to the sidewalks with candy wrappers
crinkling under the scuffed soles
of his slick crimson boots, offering
strangers a courteous cowboy nod.

He has time to order coffee, forgetting
the little cardboard sleeve
as he breathes in the warm roasted
air without windows bursting
with bodies of villains or victims.

His sense of responsibility is diffused,
his apathy thick as the atmosphere
that presses down on him and his fellow
pedestrians as they shuffle
to the beat of the orange hand
that blinks, blinks, blinks.

He is no one's savior—just a guy
with an inexplicable taste for spandex
and monograms. He finds the jingle
of car keys delightful, and in his dreams
he has deep, infinite pockets
to hold them.

He forges many friendships and beds
dark-haired reporters without
any concern for megalomaniacal bald men
or native Kryptonian juggernauts.

When Superman dreams, he dreams
of blessed mediocrity. If only the city
would sleep too.

Collin Kelley

WONDER WOMAN

The day I told my parents I wanted to trade in
G.I. Joe for Wonder Woman must have set off alarms.
I wanted to surrender my guns for the golden lasso;
more than the dolls, mind you, I wanted to *be*
Wonder Woman.
I don't remember who stitched the costume:
blue underwear with glued-on stars, a red bustier
wrapped around my seven-year-old sunken chest,
the golden eagle oddly deflated,
the headband and bullet-deflecting cuffs made
of cardboard and the length of rope my father had
spray-painted gold in the yard hooked at my side.
I lassoed my poor dad first, demanded the truth,
but there was no magic in those rough, twisted fibers.
If the rope could have squeezed out an ounce
of what he was really thinking,
I would have been dressed up as Superman or Batman,
a manly cape flying out behind me as I ran
around the backyard, hidden from the neighbors,
while my dad devised a way to build
Wonder Woman's invisible plane.

Jason McCall

SUPERMAN WATCHES LOIS LANE PULL WEEDS

Yes, I am lucky; I'll never have to die
on a treadmill, starve
myself into a cocktail dress. It doesn't matter
if I wear a seatbelt or stare into the heart
of the sun (It's just a dark lump, really).
That's why I offer to cut onions, tackle
the wasp nests and ant hills
after I save Flash and Atom
from the latest Red Tornado rebellion.
I can't know what it's like on all fours, gagging
from the bleaches that won't take
away the soy sauce stain no matter
how much grit and teeth-grinding
you put into the scrub pad.
When you woke up to your list of chores
scratched through and done, it wasn't me
shitting on your values, your *labor*
omnia vincit motto that carried
you through grad school and carries you
to the broom closet or the Windex
when I grab my cape and promise you the world
won't be torn apart by War-
world or reformed by Luthor
and his Kryptonite schemes. But my promises can't
be prophecies, darling.
That's the one power I've never had.

Ross White

Dr. Manhattan Examines His Faith

Through trial and error, the body of knowledge swells
as seas through turbulent times, with the ferocity
Greeks assigned to their Gods, though some, like Ptolemy,
correctly surmised the placement of stars propels
the elements. Millions of people are kneeling in prayer,
some facing Mecca, some facing an altar, each asking
favors of this absence. They are asking for a truth revealed,
that some new knowledge appear, without trial, without error.
They are desperate for a puppetmaster behind the string
theories, the hadrons and helixes, the intrinsic field.
I am now studying the universe's atomic response to belief,
studying people, dust mites, ash trees. I see complex reactions,
chemical eventualities, interpreted as divine action,
no more acted upon than molecules pushed by the falling leaf.

A. Van Jordan

THE ATOM AND HAWKMAN DISCUSS METAPHYSICS
DC Comics, April-May, 1969, #42
"When Gods Make Madness"

A:
a sign in the sky
a Brahman poses as a friend
a new enemy

H:
A Brahman without spirit? To defend
Against imposters of souls, to save others,
We must guard our own souls from this fiend.

A:
foes hide on borders
look behind you   nothing
in front   villains as brothers

H:
My planet exists far beyond, orbiting
Around a different sun where my wings
Seem common. Villains, friends the same—all vibrating.

A:
vibrations of kings
flutter of gnats   both pests
for both   alarms ring

H:
How do we trust what we hear, and not test
What we see? Shadow and light both reflect
The same bodies, worlds of tension and rest.

A:
what do you detect
in my voice if not knowledge
of you and respect

H:
Sometimes I forget: comforts do privilege.
I question what I know and mysteries,
Too, which keeps me safe, but ruins my pledge.

A:
no fear   a series
of challenges helps the hand
to unmask faces

H:
Unveiling spirits takes a soulful plan.
Foes challenging the world is a constant
We can depend on.

Sarah Lindsay

SUPERMAN IN SUNGLASSES

Little Clark, scuffing the toes of his Keds in the dirt,
lost in boredom wide as Nebraska, looked down.
Saw a pebble pinned under the arch of his foot,
saw earthworms tinily mouthing their way grain by grain,
tyrannosaur bones, articulate, spine strained back,
a seething fiery darkness of molten rock,
and the chipped red-painted sole of a Chinese clog.

Then the other sky. Wherever he looked after that for weeks
he saw space, the black outer space behind even the sun.
Needing to watch girls, he tried not to burn when he peeked
but saw past her underwear, past her secret skin
to viscera, ribs, and the writhing of her heart.
And saw a first egg begin its calm descent
before his steely focus came apart.

Later, with glasses, with practice by accident mostly,
he saw how his dried parents wanted him bound,
changing their tires forever, how compact Lois
was an angular mess of desire, and looking down
from Metropolis windows saw onion-skin slides stained
with lurid angers, gloating, love in vain,
the black familiar nodules in a villain's brain.

Now the curved lens's magnified rainbow reflection
shows him straggling eyebrow hairs, the step of the crow
on one side, the stare half an inch away
of his open blue-black blank eye.

P. Andrew Miller

Aquaman

Okay, I know I'm not *him,*
I can't fly to the moon in a
blue and red streak
or squeeze diamonds from coal
or bench press Lois Lane
and the rest of the *Daily Planet.*
I can't fry an egg by looking at it
or peer into the women's locker room
from the next city over.

What do I do?
I "talk" to fish,
from the tiniest plankton
to the magnificent blue whale.
Now granted, starfish do not make good conversation
And sharks speak only in Blood and Food.

But can he hear the histories of the world
told in the humpback's song?
Can he hear the jokes made in a porpoise's squeak?
Can he see the hunting dance of the anglerfish
as it swims in the darkest depths
or enjoy the bioluminous waltz of the jellyfish
on the subtle Pacific currents?

No, I'm not him.
But who said I wanted to be?

Marta Ferguson

ORACLE ON CANARY

Dear readers, you'd love that wouldn't you?
All her muscled limbs entangled with
my useless legs, my deadly slender arms.
Making out or hair pulling, it's all
double your pleasure, double your fun.
Hate to tell you, if Canary and I ever do
get into it that intimately, it'll be over
fast and end with my corpse on the floor.

Not that I'm without defenses, bum legs
or no, I can hold my own. It's that
Canary's damn dangerous. And nobody
understands that, except me and maybe Shiva.
Dinah could kick Bruce's ass in a minute.
But she wouldn't. For all her bad-ass
JLA glory days, she's always held back.
Refused to enter that bat-infested
inner darkness, won't wrap it around her
like Shiva does, cultivate it as I have.

She and Dick have got that restraint
in common. Ollie, poor fool, used to think
it weakness and paid accordingly.
I've done my own share of underestimating
and not just with Canary. That impulse
of mercy—the province of real strength—
has always eluded me. Too much to prove:
tagalong bat or crip crusader,
I've never felt I was enough.

Canary knows she is though, knows
in every fight that what's beneath her
has a life of its own, one she holds
inviolate and not because of any oath
or code, but because it is within her power
to grant divine pardon equal to the killing
she could unleash if she chose.

Her strength, light-born and absolute,
is what nobody knows and perhaps
it's that would keep her off me
if we came to blows.

John F. Buckley & Martin Ott

WITH THIS RING

I make a vow to almost-hairless father figures,
wed to a lantern bride, transformed into a storm
trooper for guardians that are walking bottles.

I am able to turn my imagination into things,
a child's wish fulfillment flung across space
until I become a floating statue, living doll.

I soar, a viridian jet stream, by force of will,
through all but golden skies, wondering when
the light of yellow suns will send me tumbling.

I trim an alien neighbor's ruby lawn with giant
emerald shears, helping to preserve private
property values, a galaxy's prime virtue.

I spray venom onto my enemies, and my lovers
don't fully trust that I will not fly away to save
my skin from vulnerability. I am never naked.

I sequester my fear in the deepest of cells, all
that would make lesser beings gibber miserably
in the vast yawn of space, feeling vectors splay.

I dream of another place, one where willpower
will not clench tightly around breasts and moons,
where shadows flicker from outside my shield.

I accessorize a uniform to make myself unique,
to sneak in my humanity, a mere popcorn kernel
caught in the green craw of a great cosmic law.

I sometimes wonder if I am the fist or the hand,
the pain of being a being breeding light and blight.
We cannot rule thoughts that do not ring through.

Curtis L. Crisler

BLACK TO BLACK

responding to Adrian Matejka's Luke Cage

These things you say come to me like arrows,
so I am caught in the lack of translation, maybe,
but if I were bulletproof, I would let all mess roll
on ground, fancy at that bounce, hot bulletshells.
Power, I must wear a suit to be Black Panther.
Power, I could still be peeved I had to change
my rep to *Black Leopard* just to offset bad press
of Rapp Brown and Huey suffocating world in
how to identify brownness. Don't sweat small
rut. Man, the economy has our spandex in bunch.
Wakanda's not the U.S., and heroes come and go—
many turning vigilante, many dealing with identity
in this age of establishing a name. I wonder if
Waku went through any of this? Power, don't
fret the sidekick—redress on new threads, Texas
and all its Texasness.
                                    Try being prodigal King,
the brother with Ororo, still fighting ritual, decrees,
sick new philosophies. I used to kick a cape, but
I'm not The Vision, right. Madness has us on lock.
Negroes can't grow 'froes without being politico.
It is hard to see with Iraq and Afghanistan—folks
fighting to hold on to smoke and mirrors, minerals
only the earth owns. Remember how we got James
Brown out of that Nixon mess? Most only think
of us as Marvel lackeys—the myths, the fictations,
the counterbalances with DC. Recognition is like
pointing out a specific ant from outer space—will
not happen without superpowers, right. At least
Daniel has your rear. (Ha!) I never thought I would
see the day a black man kicks it with pale sidekick.
FABTABULOUS!
                        ^^^^
            To me, you're holding your blue
too tight. Power, I grew up spinning inside of my

brain too. Why you hovering inside, contradicting
what you know as truth? Mama used to say, *you
will have to work twice as hard.* Why fight funk?
Do you! Be you! Work you! Everything else is
just antics—reality TV—ratings. You know this
Luke. Until next time. Ororo sends her love.

Stay hungry, *T'Challa*

Oscar McNary

NEIL

after Daemond Arrindell

Neil Gaiman animates the Sandman in a glossy
comic. Neil Gaiman is the Dream King. He uncorks terror, a
ship in a bottle. Without snapping a timber, tips it sailing
on imagination. Neil Gaiman orchestrates a massacre
at the local diner. He carves out the bluest orbs
to feed eye-socket teeth. After the
last page, Neil Gaiman returns
the light, assures me
the serial killers'
convention is
over. The
switch
flips,
but the
story sticks.
The Sandman's
frame shrinks, and we
we are peering out the same
iris and pupil. I am no less the
dreammaker, Tetrising nightmares
into my waking, before unlocking my
rented corner of unconscious. The tenement
houses everything with a cerebrum: mice and cats
and humans. Other sleepers lean in, shadowing the
wax-paper partitions. Where dreamskin can't reach,
Neil Gaiman is the current and the copper wire it
travels,   signaling shared desire. So, in the
seamless Dreaming, we are Endless.

Amy MacLennan

TINFOIL AND TWISTY-TIES

Barbie had an assortment of Kens,
a Malibu dream house,
more clothes with tulle
than a girl could wear.
She needed something more:
red bathing suit, blue underwear,
pink boots. Paint for blots of stars,
a yellow Rorschach eagle to cover
those upright mannequin breasts.
It should have been gold
for the crown, cuffs, belt,
but instead Reynolds Wrap silver
on top of ties from last week's bread.
She became a wonderful female:
protector of Madges, Francies,
G.I. Joes. There should have been
a pair of glasses, some black hair dye
for her Diana side, but she had to make do
with a hat and dark shoes.
Plastic goddess, ever-smiling bombshell doll,
the tinfoil never came off.
You settled into a woman
filled with wonder. *How does*
it happen? Why me
in this thinning slice of life?
You might have liked
a different costume.
Marilyn? Frida? Sylvia?
Still, you knew how they played
in the end. You stayed
with your invisible plane,
magic rope. You're a hero,
not a martyr, forever fresh-skinned
with tippy-toe feet. You can smile
and dazzle and shine,
and maybe save some Skippers
in the end.

Pat M. Kuras

BRANDON AND BRUCE LEE

martial arts
jeet kune do
scissors
your arms and legs
cut thru air
strong dedicated men
where would your
passion go
were it not
for the art
of fighting
without fighting
Chinese nova men
you've left us
watching empty skies

Rae Armantrout

PREVIEWS

AMERICA

The playboy scion of a weapons company repents. His company, he sees now, is corrupt, his weapons being sold (behind his back) to strong men. Alone, he builds a super weapon in the shape of a man. Now, more powerful and more innocent than ever, he attacks.

HAPPENING

The train halts. An engineer tells us we're stopped because we've lost touch with the outside world. Things are happening ahead, but we don't know what they are. *This* could represent an act of war. We stand in a field, no longer passengers.

Evelyn Deshane

TRANSFORMATIONS

Anne Sexton retold fairy tales
for fun, at first, and then for money
she pulled them out through the tips of her teeth
and kept them like a mystery
lodged inside of herself
farther back than Jonah in the whale,
farther back than the unknown soldier in ice.

when Anne became a mother,
she changed her clothing, her stories
made up disguises and new lies
told them to her babies swaddled in blankets
and kept away Rumpelstiltskin at the door.

her daughters grew up
they moved to New York, and fell in love
with men who changed their clothing in phone booths
who hid their gadgets in a cave
and who killed the bright spiders for them in the bathroom
without screaming, without complaint.

they liked men with business suits and disguises
not shoemakers, not men who wanted
straw spun into gold; they wanted heroes at night
and the men wanted back the first robin of spring
their sidekicks in the kitchen.

when her daughters grew up
and their mother wandered into the oven
willingly, like the witch in Hansel and Gretel
they went to the funeral and wondered why
a kiss would not awaken the smallest amount of grief
they wondered what ashes to ashes meant
and why they had not heard that story before.

now, they are asked by their own babies
where their stories came from
why the fascination with men in glass cases
why the women with wings and gold bracelets
why logos and tights and vigils at night
and they can only smile and look back to Anne
who led them down the magical paths
of transformations and lies.

Dana Koster

MAGIC ESCAPES US

You could never be the wolf I wanted—
clocks keep chiming noon instead of midnight,
my stubborn slippers refuse to fall off.
And maybe it's true that after this long
magic escapes us, that all the portals
to Narnia closed when we bought that first
IKEA wardrobe. I don't care. I want
the mundane adventures of this mundane
life with you. I want the woodsman's solid
arms, the fire stoked slow every morning.
Magic gone. My red hood, hidden for good.
I'll be Tony Stark with his weird goatee.
You be my Batman, the hero I need.

Sherry Stuart-Berman

LEAP

for Jack

I leap to bend you back
peel you off, but you cry
and say—as any four-year old
alive would—*the brain*
has sticky hands
and holds on holds on.
You want to stretch long
tick fast like seconds
on a clock and sit upon
the throne and do
what is right.

I want to break your grip—
fling it hard, hear it snap
past our tender cord, mother-rib;
past Batman-chain
and noisy bath-time,
the birthday game of stay-
and-be-my-gift.

I will eat metal stars, you warn.
Yes, and in your belly grow
an Iron Man immense:
Crash! my airborne rage
Slam! this bound, itchy
love-shine
into easier ground.

It is a given beautiful B for Boy:

You are brief, bullet, emBlazoned;
you will outrun my giving try.

Nicola Waldron

FURTHER ADVENTURES OF SUPERMAN

So this drunk rolls up the train, sits close,
starts waving at me, shouting LOUD—
so I get nervous—him, his breath's
all fogged, and so I say,
"Hey, leave me alone!"
(I've been here before: know
how it goes.)
But he's got no English,
gets real mean—
then
this
guy in a two-piece
comes raging down the car,
stands between me and Bullfrog,
cool as iced milk, says,
"Are you all right?"
All right? The guy's got his back
to Jack Daniels and he's looking
at *me*!
I get up with him, of course,
walk down the carriage,
all damsel-in-distress-like,
and I say, "Thank you."
Thank you.
Then he gives me this old knight-in-shining look,
and when we get back to his place, I
tear off that jacket and those polyester pants
and there's a goddamned *hero* underneath. Yes—
Superman wears a gray suit, baby:
Superman takes the same train home
as you.

Kevin Rabas

SPIDER-MAN

With Peter Parker, the change
   comes from a spider bite—
the small smart guy
   becomes strong, scales walls,
   dodges punches, punches back.
In seventh grade, I'm a runt, 5'2",
   but with poems I catch Donna's eye,
   her fist full of flowers;
I run and jump, grow 7 inches in a year,
swift past the track star in gym, when Donna,
   collecting flowers, watches me run.
I go out for basketball, stand under the rim,
   jump, tip the ball in, & we win,
& we win, & and we win. For one year,
   we're stars; I'm tall; my body catches up
with that desire to lift, dunk, return to earth
   like a satellite, like a meteor (hot rock), like a man
who can sail down to sidewalk
   held by the strand of a web, and from that hand:
spinnerets.

Steven D. Schroeder

X

When we first saw beneath
each other's clothes, we knew it
made us superheroes. We mutated
lava into *love* and vice versa.
Conjured by our kisses, binding
contracts demanded we seal
the deal daily. We sealed letters
under *adamantium* and *antarctic*
but still didn't hide our secret
identities in the signatures,
Sugarbomb and *Hugaton*.
With our gifts, we manufactured
stellar pornography and graphs
of our momentum and place
in space-time. Then we settled
into a rental unit with central air,
where *relight the pilot* was no longer
an entendre for our talents.
The ability to double sunrises
with sexiness cooled into a knack
for baking cookies *sooooo goooood*,
the neighbors said. While playing
Tedium one Friday game night,
the Answerer, who foresaw a future
of same nights counted out
as cutlery, guessed nothing but
zip and *void*. The inevitable breakup
of the universe soon followed.
Impotent to stop it, we froze
home movies on that frame
where it became clear how special
effects allowed us to appear
on fire again. We crossed our eyes
out with booze to unsee the *why*
science couldn't reason. At the end
of dating diaries, we found our power
was wishing we could turn
the planet backward to before
our flames transformed to *former*.

Laurel Maury

Love Song for Marvin the Martian

How I loved the sweeping ships of light
raining destroying legions down
on guns that shot forever
into the TV night
of my Atari skies!

At NASA, computers purred past supper
as Von Braun's disciples stared into screens,
and Dad punched numbers,
furious at the modem, calling Houston,
not his falling-down house.

I was a child in a pixel sea,
defending the world with quarters,
or dropping the joystick to watch it die.
I loved my tiny, honest mad scientist
with his aim to improve the view,

by blowing it all to Kingdom Come:
thoughts as pure as Pac-Man's hunger.
You lacked the false guilt of adults
I never believed in. My faith lay
in burying action figures,

trusting the earth to save them
—Luke, Leia, G.I. Joe, Batman
deep in soil beneath my window.
All destructions are offerings
prayers bizarrely wrong.

Oh pretty one, you're God gone mad,
and the end of the world looks as fun
as Space Invaders, as The Caverns of Mars,

a Hannah-Barbara cubist jungle
of scaffold-traps in paths to the sky

where, with you, I'll have the thrill
of vast, score-carded body counts,
cities of millions winking out.
I'll have again, at each game's end,
that divine instant when the world goes boom.

Alison Stone

A Bird! A Plane! A Frog!

After the mad scientist is foiled,
his bomb buried so deep in the earth
its explosion hurts no one but Underdog,
my daughter, naïve to movies, sees
the limp beagle and pleads,
He's not dead, Mom, is he?
This is a remake, so Underdog's a real pooch—
no job shining shoes, no secret energy pill,
though this was later cut
to keep kids with superhero dreams
from gobbling their parents' medications.
TV now shows preschool beauty queens amp up on Pixie Stix;
one mom serves her toddler
a mix of Red Bull and Mountain Dew.
Yesterday Lance Armstrong told Oprah
he doped for every win.
The second-place finishers won't get the Tour de France titles—
they took steroids, too. Is it cheating
to hold the camera so long on the motionless hound
my daughter starts to sob, though every grown-up knows
his eyes will flicker open
for a happy ending and a sequel?
In my favorite episode, Simon
traps them in a tank and lets it fill. Worn out,
Underdog stands around spouting poetry
while sweet Polly Purebred dives
again and again to the bottom of the rising water.
If at first you fail your deed…
Travis Tygart spent years and taxpayer millions
to prove Armstrong lied.
We want our heroes humble and lovable,
though Shoeshine pines hopelessly for Polly. He can't compete
with his own superpowered self.
Speed of lightning, roar of thunder
How our lives
swelled with possibility when he defeated death
and soared over mountains—
eyes bright with dollar signs and American flags.

Campbell McGrath

HUNGER

1

This is a true story. One day when I lived in Manhattan, burglars broke
into my apartment and stole my tape deck, my raincoat, and my Incredible
Hulk piggybank. I was having a party that night; Bruce and Mike and I had
trudged all the way down from 116th Street lugging cases of Genessee beer,
bottles of bourbon and tequila, sacks of ice, but as soon as we opened the
door I knew.

So.

Briefly, we cursed the perpetrators; we put the beer on ice and discovered
the loss of the raincoat, an inexplicable theft; we called the police, who
were too busy to trouble with us. And that was it. All in all, Bruce and
Mike took it harder than I did, though it had nothing really to do with
them. My main concern was this: now we would have to find another tape
deck for the party. Beyond that, I was strangely unconcerned. It was only
things, after all, part of the shell game of material possessions, albeit vital
possessions, my tape deck being my primary source of entertainment in
those days, music my constant companion, whatever songs obsessed me
that week played over and over in a kind of religious-ecstatic frenzy. But
Crazy Eddie was full of new tape decks—Crazy Eddie was solvent back
then—and the two hundred bucks it would cost was an inconvenient but
not impossible loss to sustain. I was working at the 79th Street boat basin as
a carpenter, dockhand, watchman; my dad was helping pay for graduate
school; student loans took care of the rest. If the banks were unaware I was
spending their borrowed money on tape decks and tequila, what fault was
that of mine? If I was unaware how long the albatross of debt would hang
from my neck, what fault was that of the banks?

2

As to the culprit, I had my suspicions: George, the superintendent, a
notorious drunk with a passkey, to whom I'd given a fifth of vodka at
Christmas and perhaps this was my thanks in return; Mona, the "model"
who lived above me, whose hands-on sagas of needy desperation rung
more than a few false notes; the scabrous crackheads living in a broken-
down van around the corner, a jacked-up, fire-streaked vehicle we called

the Mobile Crime Lab—drugs, guns, what didn't they sell out the back
of that van? Whoever they were, the burglars had come and gone by
the window. Halfway down the fire escape is where we found the Hulk,
abandoned in midheist, a green plastic figurine stamped out by the
millions at some factory in China, icon of a frugality beyond my needs or
practice, a dead weight of dozens of pounds of pennies.

3

At the party we got drunk and listened to loud music on a walkman
jury-rigged through my speakers. A famous poet stood on the bed and
left dirty footprints all over my pillow. In the morning I slept late, tidied
up, feeling hung over and world weary. In the afternoon I went to work,
carried lumber, hammered nails out along the seawall on the Hudson, sat
in the little guard shack come evening, buzzing people through the security
gate, excluding those who did not belong, until the late-shift guy arrived
at midnight, a lovely, heavily-armed Nigerian named Afaso. What I did
next speaks volumes: I went home. I was hungry, had eaten nothing since
breakfast, but I was also broke, having blown it all on the party, two dollars
in my pocket until payday.

Now wait: certainly I could have put my hand on some money with a
phone call, borrow whatever I needed from friends, easily, as a matter of
course. But I was taking a kind of Spartan pleasure in my poverty that day,
my straitened circumstances indulged as a badge of honor, a penance for
my losses,

and so I walked the thirty blocks home, fell into bed, and dreamt

that my skin was the color of money.

Everything was backwards: I was stiff with rage when I was supposed to
be calm;

I was Lou Ferrigno, but I was supposed to be Bill Bixby.

At the edge of consciousness I could see him, my alter ego, hard at work, typing up scientific formulae, sitting at my desk, in my apartment, but I could not get to him, could not transform back into that version of myself.

My will blew in the wind like shredded paper, a swirling confetti of dollar bills.

I smoked a cigarette and lit fire to my poems. A woman came through the window and put them out while I watched. I paid her money. I slept with her. I was hungry. I was helpless.

I woke near tears.

4

Though it was ten years ago, that dream was one of the most vivid in my life, and I remember it plainly. This year, for the first time, I've started to make money in a reasonable way, a "professional" way. I'm a husband, a father, an assistant professor at the state university. I drive to work in a red station wagon along boulevards of shoe stores and fast food restaurants like any other citizen, like the Joe Taxpayer I have become, a transition from student days that seems profound but really isn't. I'm still in debt, still paying off the borrowed leisure of those apprentice years, but I have never seriously lacked for anything material in my life: in times of relative poverty, I have lived happily poorer; in relative wealth, much the same. Those days on 105th Street I was no more than an interloper, a transient passing through to another life. For all that it was a testament to my buried fears and desires, the secret currency of power and helplessness, bright coins in dark waters, I can see, looking back, that the dream of the Incredible Hulk had little even to do with me, with my life as it would develop, a Polaroid taking on shape and color, rising and brightening away from those mean streets. It was for those from whose shoulders the burdens would not be so easily lifted, those whose deprivation was more than a caprice: for Afaso, the night watchman, in the quiet hours before dawn; for George, the super, drunk again in the basement when the boiler needs fixing; for the junkies, the gypsy cabbies, the street-corner boys in front of the bodega; for those who would steal pennies in their desperation, who violated the sanctity of my small world, who came back three weeks later to take the stereo tuner, the last bottle of tequila, and the piggybank Hulk—again!—this time successfully, stamping out their cigarette butts on my floor, not even bothering with the window but walking in and out the front door and leaving it open behind them.

This is a true story.

This is a dream, a poem, a song, a prayer.

This is for all those trapped within the body of desire. This is for all those fleshed with the alien muscle of need.

This is for all those who would walk the avenue and say

I am sufficient in the sunlight and mercy of this day, I will have none of what you offer, no longer does my marrow ache with wanting, I crave for nothing, though I am hungry I shall hunger no more.

Lorraine Schein

COMIC BOOK CONFIDENTIAL

It's a toy relationship,
A comic book love.

You make me feel like Brenda Starr
Or Lois Lane, rescued for the umpteenth time, by Superman
As she falls yet again to her death
From a tall Metropolis skyscraper,
The buildings below looming ominously closer.
Betty and Veronica (mostly Veronica),
Lori Lemaris, Superman's first girlfriend, Atlantean mermaid,
And Wonder Woman.

The Comics Code would never approve us:
On the splash page, I ink in the colors
That first night at your place—
My curry-red skirt from Guatemala on your bed,
Just my red Tibetan beads left on;
Your arms, the hiding place.

Later, you handed me a single white flower
White as Orphan Annie's eyes.
I was as wet between my legs
As the rain drifting through your windows—
And the scent of African violet still lingered
From the tiny bottle we found at
The street vendors on Broadway and 8th.

In the next panel,
Your apartment glows, mysterious and dark
Like Dr. Strange's townhouse in the heart of the Village.

I want to be in your every panel,
Written into your script—
Squirrel to your Moose,
O Master of the Mystic Arts.

I'll supply the thought balloons,
You supply the word balloons.
It's a Marvel special, a DC double issue,
All my toasters are straying.

It's a comic book relationship,
A toy love.

Collin Kelley

TO MARGOT KIDDER, WITH LOVE

I spent the summer of 1980 with Margot Kidder,
made her my surrogate on those hot Friday afternoons
when my mother would dump me at the movie theatre,
flying off to her other life faster than Superman.

They all knew me at the counter, asking
for the same ticket every week. I smiled,
perfected my act of comic book geek,
but even those indifferent teenagers had x-ray vision.

In the dark, I mouthed the dialogue
like a Shakespearean tragedy as Margot Kidder
beamed down at me from the undercarriage
of an Eiffel Tower elevator commandeered
by terrorists, jumped into the raging Niagara River,
hung from wires for hours as she pretended to fly.

I pretended not to care what my mother was doing,
but I was cashing in part of my childhood to keep up
the charade, as she tucked money in my pocket
for popcorn and a strange phone number
where she could be reached in case of emergency.

Margot Kidder eased me through rising panic
every Friday at 1 p.m. as I was deposited
on the sidewalk and mother's car shimmered
like a disappearing mirage, moving bullet time
away from me.

Margot Kidder was Lois Lane.
Feisty, brave, stubborn, in perpetual need of rescue.
Her dark hair, un-PC cigarette dangling,
whiskey voice, in love with the one man
she could never truly have.

Years later, when she had her publicized breakdown,
was found dirty and wandering the streets,
I cried in front of the TV, wishing I could give her
even a fragment of the comfort she gave me
when I was ten and in need of rescue.

Stephen Burt

SCENES FROM NEXT WEEK'S *BUFFY THE VAMPIRE SLAYER*

The rolls of carpet come out in all colors:
Apparently unsalable, they lean
Against the Sunnydale Tool
And Magic Shop—then up
In smoke they go: show the whole block on fire,
Then cut to Faith, who's smiling. She's to blame.
And here come the credits. Later the star of the show

Could arrive, see vamps, warn all, stand out,
Snap a fence post in half, and start
To fence with it. O foleys, do your work:
We want to be half-fooled. That good can win
And isn't always ugly, that sleek fish
Were athletes once, werewolves play Fender Strats
And souls are round like geodes inside-out

Has to be true for these dusty particulars
To be like somewhere we would choose to live:
Otherwise the closed shop is, simply, closed
For good and business reasons, morning made
Of risible schedules, babysitting and cash,
The script not censored or altered after all
But the work of a number 2 pencil moving along

With several thousand others in their wooden
Tiers on Saturday, blackening
Old questions that arrange us for our roles
In plots no TV shows, on the narrow channels
Nobody would choose, if she thought she could have a choice.

Barbara Griest-Devora

TRUE HEROINE BECOMES ANNOYED AT BEING THE ONLY FEMALE SUPERHERO

And who wouldn't be, those square chins always poking
you in the head, impossibly large shoulders blocking
your view of everything you know to be feminine

and every waist in the room smaller than your own.
On her uniform, she has the INE in
HeroINE blown up to twice the normal size

so there's no mistake, grows her hair extra long
and picks out a scalloped cape. She wants
patent leather boots that exude "female" down

to their spiked heels and sticks out her breasts
for no reason but to point out she has them.
It's way past time to hire more girls for this gig

but all she can find are mothers with diaper bags
and business girls with clunky heels.
It's that she hates to be a token anything, wants

to teach these heroes a thing or two about women
that they never even saw coming and when it's there,
they'll be feverish and undecided. It's always the same:

after flying practice, she cleans up alone in showers
decidedly inferior, misses out on the ribbing and slapping
of backs. It was enough to make a heroine go mortal.

But you never knew: maybe one day, she'd join them
in these showers, watch as the water beaded and ran
down legs, as soap foamed down skin, slid

down elbows. No one would have to notice:
she'd hide in a corner so dark God hardly knows,
keep her hands and slender fingers to herself.

Quincy Scott Jones

SUPERHERO PARTY

Captain Cold Front copped a smooth pad for a superhero with a pension plan. It was my understanding that the real money was in vigilante work: business jerks who fight crime most nights, secure merchandising rights and make a killing on the side. Hide their identities and their earnings then retire in style. Meanwhile, federal superheroes file a 401K. But Cold Front, he must have been doing okay: modern split-level with a view of the bay, large backyard with a water-feature pool; definitely a cool place to throw the party of the year. You know, mostly an office thing, but everyone's here: Major Mercy and Johnny Long-Arm, Destiny Man and Adam Bomb, the Black Under II and the umpteenth White Hope; everyone you know — American Pi and Flaming Hetro—all those who follow Status Quo. Status Quo even showed up for hour or so. He's the worst of them all, with his bulging broad shoulders and super square jaw. How can any of us live up to him? Our capes don't blow in the wind even when we're standing still. Still, it was good to see him before he flew off to save the moon. We all mosey off to the saloon wet bar and assorted dessert trays save for a few like yours truly who's making his way to the canopy only to discover a superheroine shooting heroin into the back of her knee.

"Don't judge me," she says putting a cap on the needle's head, "You never led a team to their probable deaths, flew straight into the fiery mess: burning civilians holding what's left of their bodies, screaming like nobody can hear them. I hear them. I'm first on the scene. And I've seen things, man: monster and machine; radiation and poisoned skin turn green; bullets burn as they broke open bone; a child in shock standing all alone; smoldering rumble that used to be *Home*. So, you know, I start feeling not so good. My stomach turns and shakes and I put the team at risk. So I go to my superior, he tells me to take this. My shakes go away, and I'm back to save the day. Do it all while wearing lingerie. Stomp the villain while onlookers holler and hoot." She slips her kit back into her boot. "You see, we're the good guys and the good guys always win. Then we got to get up the next day and do it all over again. So tell me, am I wrong?"

She smiles at my silence and puts her mask back on.

Kim Roberts

NOT-SO-SUPER HEROES

Edema Man can make others swell at will
so their rings no longer fit.
Dustball Man distracts foes
with repetitive domestic chores.
Each spring thaw, Ice Damage Man
reveals new potholes along your daily commute.
Papercut Man leaves his enemies with cruel,
nearly invisible hand wounds.
Digital Signal Man can jam
all high-speed internet connections.
Existential Man paralyzes enemies
with a desire to read Heidegger.

Keith S. Wilson

Robotto Mulatto

I am the Robotto Mulatto
The day walker, the glimmer in the night
I am the ambiguous apparition
        shifting colors like a conch shell
I am the Halfrican Hulk
The onerous Oreo who will not reveal
        where these big lips come from

I am more than meets the eye
My skin separates along perfect tan seams
        lifts with a hydraulic hiss
        flips in on itself
        and transforms cultures
My skin is controlled like a remote
        with the styling of my hair
        I shift color circuits
        first mustached Mexican, now bearded Egyptian,
        maybe the mysterious collage of whatever
        your half-cousin is

My words are double-edged knives,
I can say things that you can't say
        because I have one foot in your door
        and another go-go gadget foot in someone else's
And when all else fails I have a race card
        up each sleeve.

My life is a tug of war between
        being fully Clark Kent and Superman
I don't understand the master/slave jumpers
        on my hard drive
Can't fully hug or hate my white motherboard
My weakness is that Silicon Valley
        isn't big enough for the idea of me,
        and that around here things move so fast
        that before the world is ready for me
        I'll have already become obsolete

Jed Myers

AUTUMN'S PLAIN FATE

I'm not waiting for Halloween.
I'm donning the electric-blue bodysuit of Dragonfly Man—it's erotically
tight, tighter than skin—in the shade
of a mountain towering over a lake
where thousands of dragonflies mate.
And I'll go skimming over the waste
on wings of spider-silk and dandelion
paste, defying Einstein and Dante,
till I come face-to-face
with the tall mirrors of Love's Lost City,
where my wind-waxed hair will unfurl
in lonely wide curls like Salvador Dali's,
my ex-wife will see and come track me
down in her lasciviously tubular sedan,
and I'll leap, in a quick quantum quip
that tickles the bosons, to a rooftop
and blind her by the afternoon glare
off the green gems of my eyes,
till she cries out the thin gin of her fear,
trips out of her car, and offers
herself her own forgiveness. Neither
one of us was ever an insect
any more than the other. Neither
one of us could mate in the air
nor iridesce in the shadow-light
on a lake in late August. All this, just
to free us up to an autumn's plain fate,
to wander the shapes of the lovely dust,
at last—to separate.

Jessie Carty

Fat Girl: The Superhero

You won't be Wonder Woman
because you wouldn't wear
that outfit. Although, when
you were five, and not fat
you had those red boots
that you swore made you run faster.

Your least favorite is Super Girl,
the girl, the skirt, how close the word
Super is to Supper and how you'd fall
out of the sky targeting
the first red Wendy's sign.

Maybe you could be the awkward/
obscure Gigantic Girl whose gift
was growing tall, not out you notice,
but up. She was hefty, having
strength and size like a man.

Lesley Wheeler

MANIFESTO

The fate of the multiverse will be decided through
a climactic battle between Poetry Karma Woman—
hips thrown into fortunate shadow
by her quilt-cape—and Judge-O-Tron, who knows
that only perfectly controlled power wins.
He is her kryptonite and she the object of his most fragrant
envy while sipping cognac every evening in a crystal-
glitter unassailable alpine fortress of literary merit.
She lives comfortably in the valley but suspects
her work is smudged, the fusion reactor embedded
in each stanza steadily, fatally leached of force.

You say, this is fantasy's hitch: false dichotomy,
predictably gendered, then a race for resolution. But
She Who Does Unto Others lusts
for the pitiless metal god of ambition. Perhaps
there is a cottage at some alternate altitude where
they could try on each other's clothes: twinkly armor,
pouchy tights. How embarrassing for both if, despite
their oaths and alliances, the paparazzi caught them. No
one can know how she despises and deceives League
members, especially Competent Well-Connected Man
and Pretty Good Girl. How his most cryptic, brilliant
productions are true-love-letters, addressee unknown.

Barbara Griest-Devora

Ocean Man Decides He's Homesick

The one from the sea still drips
silt from his cape, can't find
a sheet big enough to cover

his longing for water. Even
when he tries to make love,
his arms flop fin-like, legs kicking

behind him, his thrusts more like
ground swells as he tries to
recall silver-haired mermaids

who once sang to him, who could
move with him to the discordant
rhythm of oceans. Now, the creaks

of small beds ruin even the memory
of any long-legged, smooth-skinned girl
thankful to be saved from Evil Wretch,

whispering her wishes to stars and heroes.
For romance, he'll speak of tall ships, pull strings
of pearls from his magic belt. "The sea, the sea,"

he'll say between villains. "The wild
virginal sea!" He stalks the streets
like a sailor, wants to hear the ocean

in the gulf air that sometimes billows
down purple city streets, prays
for this sound in the cacophonous alleys

of his new life. If there were only a wharf,
a jetty he could wait on, refusing to leave
until the very crustacean sound

like violins and the only truths on the black sea
are wishes he sends to jellyfish with tendrils
glowing like any other lying, poisonous star.

Michael Arnzen

SISTER SUPERMAN

Kryptonite, it turns out,
robbed him of his masculinity—
which was alien, anyway—
and his newfound breasts and curls
made him look awfully silly
in his bright red underwear.

But that didn't stop the villains
from beating him up, for,
being villains, they had no compunction
against hitting a girl, no matter how super.
And nobody likes a Woman of Steel.
So he, now she, donned a black robe
to cover her shame and dropped out of sight.

But her x-ray vision taunted her often
and she needed a more fashionable
fortress of solitude—the church
was conveniently located and pretty.
When she decided to become a nun,
she was welcomed into the convent
and absolved of her unimaginable sins.

Now Sister Superman wows
the girls with her feats of strength:
faster than a confession, able
to leap long pews in a single
jaunty skip and bound.
She's also handy around the abbey
and loves editing their newsletter.

Sometimes when she prays
in the silent cathedral
her chair lifts right up
up in the air and she hits

her head on the angels
painted on the ceiling.

Sometimes when the other nuns
aren't looking she changes
her costume in the confessional,
puts on makeup and remembers.
Sometimes she is God. Sometimes
she is Clark dreaming of Lois.

Sometimes she visits the local prison
and dispenses truth, the Eucharist
and—especially when no one
is looking—the American way.

Jessie Carty

GIVE ME A G!
for Melanie

Since no one has created you, I will,
even though I cannot draw a circle
that doesn't look like a pear; I must
paint you with words whether or not

it sounds cliché you will fly, Geek
Girl. Your cape, to me, is green. You
wear stylish, boxy, black frames
even though Superman offered you

laser eye surgery. You wear a "G"
on your chest, written in an Arial font.
You read minds, wear sweat pants
because it is cold inside clouds.

In your free time, you write it all down.
Your typing sounds like the last hurried
seconds of microwaving popcorn
before you know the bag is beginning

to burn. Your never ruin your snacks.
You smell the moment when the pop
is perfect. Like how your skin is perfect,
because your second secret power is

moisturizing. When you are trying
to hide the Geek Girl, you wear skirts
and contacts that change your eyes
from brown to Elizabeth Taylor purple.

You play dumb.

Cynthia Schwartzberg Edlow

SUPER DAN COMICS QUESTION BOX SERIES # 28

Super Dan: I cannot stop
an ocean. My powers, not that great.
People will come to tweezer computer parts
into your human brain. They will look
unremarkable; think of Aunt Sylvia and Uncle Hy.
All that's left is working out
the bugs. No more dwarfish screens
everyone is hypnotized by, the relentless fingertipping
like chickens scratching the earth.
Your eyes, eased into a netted hammock,
the screen itself ensconced
in the soft matter of your head.
That might take a minute for you to temple up to.
There would be no more habitual lying to yourself.
No more animal parades in retro pedal cars.
No more chips and dip. Remember
when girls wore jumpers?
Baloney on money! Stash platinum.
Watch your mirrors on that one.

        As swiftly as he bursts in
        Super Dan whooshes off¾with
        a neighbor's entreaty to corral
        one loose and testy buffalo
        skipping down the avenue.
        Folded in the pocket of his supertights,
        the week's grocery list. In his left hand,
        Saturday party clothes for the dry
        cleaners—*didn't we have a time?*—
        and from his mouth a hardware-store invective
        involving an anti-siphon valve, an elbow
        and 40-gauge PVC pipe. Don't ask.
        In his wake there is deposited
        a portentous chunk of sizzling iron ore
        from the famous center
        of the inscrutable, cutely tipsy mother earth.

Extracted, it appears, to bolt down his graph-
lined mystery papers—upon them, scribblings
pellucid and relevant,
casually covering the unembroidered mud desk
in his rather chaotic, but nevertheless

not unwelcoming, impressively two-tone, cave.

Cathryn Cofell

HERO ON THE ROOF

He ain't no fat Santa,
he ain't no G.I. Joe,
no one voted him in or out,
he just rose up,
he just climbed up
  like the original King Kong
       scaling the Empire State
  but in dazzling color, climbing
from a cave into
the cloudless noon color,
blinding! He's only three feet tall
and except for a dishtowel cape
he's naked as the trunk of a mango tree,
his body built
like a suitcase, like a carry-on bag,
he's carrying on like a rock star,
jumping and grinding,
he's yelling *yippee-ki-yay* and grinning,
a stupendous *I-just-saved-the-day* grin.
He's got a big letter *J* painted orange on his chest
and there's a piece of me that catches
when I see it, that knows this is no hero,
this is some hopped-up sports fan,
that the J is for *Jets* or *Jaguars*
and I'm sure now someone (maybe even me)
will call 911 and the sirens will wail
because he's a phony or a suicide
who might just jump,
who might not catch me if I fall.
But there's another piece of me that catches
on the J as *Justice* or *Jubilation*
if all I do is look up and believe
in all three freaky feet of him:
I will believe—*Sweet Super J*—I will,
because the alternative is much too cruel,
the alternative is the world, unsaved.

Dorianne Laux

SUPERMAN

Superman sits on a tall building
smoking pot, holding the white plumes in,
palliative for the cancerous green glow
spreading its tentacled evil beneath his
blue uniform, his paraffin skin.

The pot also calms him so he can look
down through the leafy crowns of the Trees
of Heaven to patches of black asphalt,
a small dog chained to a grate
raising his leg against a sapling.

It's 2010 and the doctors have given him
another year in Metropolis. Another year
in paradise when he's high, another year
in hell when he's not.
A magazine falls from his lap. Lois
on the cover of Fortune, the planets
aligned behind her, starlight glancing off
her steely upswept hair.

He lifts his head from his hands
as the sun sets, the sound of muffled gunfire
in every city of the world ricochets
through his gray brain. He'll take care of it
tomorrow, the thankless, endless task
of catching dirty bombs and bullets,
though like the dishes piling up in the sink
there are always more.

365 dark days left to try to gather them all,
tunnel through to the earth's core
and bury them there. But for now he leans
his wide back against the stove-hot bricks
and stretches each bluelong leg.
Blissfully stoned he doesn't notice
when his heel clips the chipped wing
of a granite angel, can't feel the Kryptonite
bending its rays up toward his scarlet heart.

R. Narvaez

THE DARK KNIGHT FALLS

I shall become a bat...later.
No, I won't go down to the gym this morning—
the dojo smells of feet.

I hate pilates.

Revenge burns in me, on the couch.
Alfred opens the curtains and the sun
shines like a clown's smile over the city.

I wonder if there is a donut in the mansion.

My origin story depresses me.
How many sit-ups, how many pushups
can ever bring Mother and Father back?

The cape is so warm like a blanket.

The cave needs a new coat of paint.
The computer needs an upgrade.
The costume needs to be let out an inch. Or two.

Catwoman never calls when I need her.

The Mark of Zorro on cable doesn't help.
I use a Batopener to open a *cerveza*.
I bite each tortilla chip into the shape of wings.

Celia Lisset Alvarez

WONDER WOMAN GOES THROUGH MENOPAUSE

Your legs have dried up,
you shift them restlessly at night
as if jumping up the sides of buildings.
You never had any children;
your legacy is all red, white, and blue.
The onlookers laugh at you now,
at your star-spangled grandma panties,
your Vegas bustier. Jiggle-thighed,
you can still outrun those hoodlums,
but you can no longer stand the truth.
That black hair now comes in a bottle,
and Diana Prince looks just as good as you,
school marmy, Lane Bryanty.
Those pointy boots have done a number
on your bones. The doctors recommend
shock absorbers made of feminim.
It's not the same, not the same.
Only the steel-blue eyes remain,
not clear but contact lensed.
Your million-dollar smile's
all caps and collagen.
It's a farce—
you just don't fit in anymore.
This morning you caught yourself thinking
Super Girl's a little whore.
Paradise Island's a resort,
nothing but wet t-shirt contests,
vomit on the floor.
You have no place,
no flag at your back.
On Halloween the little girls
dress up like Disney princesses.
You fly over them in your invisible plane,
clucking your tongue like an old woman.

Ryan G. Van Cleave

THE FLASH, IN OLD AGE

Mostly he just watches the circling ocean birds
as he sits in a porch rocker near the Pacific,
looking for blue everlasting. His childhood
friends no longer swing by to visit, being
otherwise committed. Green Lantern chases
his devil-may-care kids, Jade and Obsidian
to all ends of the earth. Wonder Woman, Dr. Fate,
Hawkman, and the rest still run the Justice
Society of America, which isn't easy thanks
to Johnny Thunder and The Black Canary
drinking the Elixir of Evil along with Grodd
and Captain Cold. Worse, the speed clones
who emerged like safety pins into the heart
of The Flash are still at work, chasing down
bullets from behind, zipping from his failing sight
like darkness lost between rocks. The Whizzer.
Quicksilver. And McSnurtle the Turtle (a.k.a.
The Terrific Whatzit). Jay Garrick—The Flash—
considered reimmersing himself in the deadly
chemical fumes that superhero-ized him as a
college sophomore, but the voice of heaven
has been calling him, promising a place without
hunger or thirst. He is confused with feeling,
forced by gravity and aching muscles at last
to ponder stillness, the particular mundane
moments that make up the wholeness of a day.
As the sun sets again, he makes quarters vanish
from his hand; semi-speedy fingers are all that's
left of the blur that was his youth. Overhead,
the stars come to life, burning at the dark as strongly
as ever. But The Flash's heart does not beat faster.

Quincy Scott Jones

THE DAY SUPERMAN DIED

The Day Superman Died

This N-word
cut me off
and I hit my breaks
thinking I should hit the
gas hit the back off his car
pull over and play dumb

N-word gets out
(big N on his chest)
"Yo B-word!
What the F-word are you doing?"

"Sorry, Brother, but I couldn't stop"

but it wouldn't stop
the pushin' the shovin' the throwing down
the comic book street fight

but brothers shouldn't be fightin'
and we shouldn't 've been slaves
and I shouldn't 've been speeding to work

but my boss's a jerk
and after one look at
me late walkin' in on the sly
He's going ask why

"Sorry, Charlie,
Thought a man could fly."

The Day Superman Died

Death took the weekend off
Two days of nightmares and
memories but no
Death

Friday
Death took Derrida
layer at a time
one system
one organ
broke down cell walls and
took Derrida from Derrida

and spent the weekend with laughter
ambassadors who thought they knew
saying, "You got Derrida.
But who got you?"

The Day Superman Died

Ray Charles played during the procession
Rodney Dangerfield gave his seat to Rosa Parks
Richard Pryor came to the podium
said "iaintdeadyetmotherfuckers"
and lit a candle for Christopher Reeve
Aaliyah sang a ballad
featuring C. Delores Tucker in a gangsta rap solo
and even Tupac phoned in from Cuba
and all my heroes were having blast
and we all sat in metal chairs
and we all got degrees from Julliard
and we all agreed America
will never be this young.

Gary Jackson

OLD LIONS

1.

Lobo and Waku down another shot
of rye at the lobby bar, knowing
they'll be passed over for every award
save maybe a lifetime achievement,
unless Luke Cage or Catwoman-
as-Eartha-Kitt win again. T'Challa,

half-drunk, buys rounds for nearby
tables, loud as he wants to be, while
the Dogs of War stand guard, each
with a powder blue pocket square
covering their hearts. Everyone is

two drinks from ejection.
Mari McCabe sings *Nice Work*
if You Can Get It, but pours
too much blue and not enough
black. It's bad comedy
Lobo quips. *A cowboy*
and a prince walk into a bar.

2.

An empty bottle of Bulleit
reminds Waku of his tribe,
long gone: their gray faces
surrendering themselves
for their hero. A reprint prince
without a kingdom. A boy
who beat his own for sales.
Might keep him in circulation,
though. Might get a reboot,
might get a Halloween costume.

3.

Most Sensational, Most Startling,
Blackest Superhero, The Hardest
Motherfucker Alive, The Realest
Negro: T'Challa wins them all. Nothing
to take home, Waku still
applauds the night's end.

4.

Lobo only wants to know who the judges are.

David Lunde

SUPERMAN *INOXYDABLE*

(D. 11-18-92 R.I.P.)

Superman died today, victim
of a world grown too alien
for his own alien virtues—
goodness & right, honesty & trust.
The days when he vanquished Nazis
in his immaculate, flag-hued, skin-tight suit
have corroded away like Metropolis itself
into a grimy cyberpunk future,
a time when observable goodness
is viewed with cynical suspicion:
we know that anyone with those
chiseled good looks and that kind of power
would be wetting that spring-steel willy,
turning our Earth girls
on his inexhaustible spike
like game-birds on a spit—
I mean, hey pal, wouldn't *you*?

No, Superman died just in time.
The boy scouts of today
are fondling the pieces in their pockets
and saving up someone else's grocery money
to buy a Mac-10 or an Uzi.
Jimmy is listening to gangsta rap
on his boombox, while Lois
is hooking on the side and watching
reruns of *Thelma and Louise.*
He just couldn't have adapted.
The Man of Steel today is Robo-Cop
or the Terminator who can rip
the still-beating heart from your body.

Still, I can't help hoping
that the Man of Steel will remain rustless
in his kryptonite tomb, that his virtue
will remain a stainless legend, that

in our time of greatest need
an earthquake will set him free
to rise again renewed

like King Arthur from the grave
and vanquish black-clad evil for us all.

John McCarthy

BETWEEN LAND AND SEA

Aquaman was turning gray and his skin was a perpetual prune, illuminated even more by the natural onset of wrinkles. He was frustrated by how slow he moved on land. When he was not swimming, it felt like a painful dream—unable to move fast enough. His body started to reject all the walking, eventually developing a galling case of plantar fasciitis. His webbed feet did not fit naturally into orthotic shoes. He just wanted to dive, dive, and die. Deep, deep down. He wanted to resign from The Justice League. His stint, his tenure, was becoming a burden and he just wanted to disappear like he did in 2006, when he resurfaced to catch his breath with a new identity.

The scales on his chest were drying out. He just sat around in the recliner at the Hall of Justice like a languorous fish out of water. He was an old man. In the night, Atlantis would warble through the murkiness into his jeweled dreams. It was like a mirror and he would see all of his essence glowing back at him from the ocean floor. Aquaman would wake up from the phantasm; instead of fish, birds and their incessant chirping. His mouth, like a hungry, confined fish, would open and close on the syllables *Po-sei-don*. The ivy growing up the Hall of Justice was beautiful, but it was not as warm as the seaweed that would wrap like breezy silk around the lost and sunken limestone of his old kingdom.

Wonder Woman took the Justice League out to dinner one night, while Aquaman stayed behind eyeing their departure anxiously. The rest of the superheroes, in their later years, had grown used to Aquaman binge drinking and watching *Planet Earth Ocean Deep* documentaries. The flickering blue television haze was not a good substitute for water, though. He thought the term "channel surfing" was an insult. The sunken ship of his nostalgia had been buried long enough. Aquaman rose and hobbled out to the garage. He lifted the keys to the Batmobile off a small table and drove, nonstop, to the Atlantic Coast. He scribbled out a thank-you note on one of many tissues Batman was starting to leave, used and crumpled, around the Hall and in costume pockets.

Aquaman limped along the beach out toward the tide. The sand becoming familiar under his thin calluses as the ocean ebbed and he receded. He felt the lightness of water pressure. Squinting and plugging his nose, he slipped under and travelled home.

Celia Lisset Alvarez

Superman Confronts Me About Dinner

Lois, he says, *I feel I've earned the right
to breakfast on pretzels and hot chocolate
if I wish, to have a deep-fried burrito
for lunch, and to follow every meal
with a pint of Licorice Cream.*

He is old, you see, the cape's hem
drags on his heels in a perpetual
threat of tripping, and his chest
is narrower than his waist.
The doctors say to keep him
on a steady diet of fruits and veggies,
steamed, preferably, and 3 oz. exactly
of wild Alaskan salmon. I think:

This is my portion, all the acclaim
of decades now lulled to a constant buzz
from his hearing aid, and my shrill voice
the one seagull cawing for his ear
on this still shore. This is what is left
to me, the steel winnowed to a fragile
husk. I once ran a pale hand
over that square jaw, I once touched
a trembling lip to that cool brow. Now
I must say *no,* and *not today.*

This is my superpower. A kind of temporal
x-ray vision, to see not what is hidden
but what is gone. I guide Superman
through the aisles at Publix, have him grip
the cart at ten and two, with the cape
safely waving in his wake like the flag
of some country that we've left but still
would die for, given the chance. When

he reaches for a package of Oreos,
I sometimes let him keep it.
We sit at the kitchen table
with two glasses of skim milk. We
separate each half, and lick the cream.

Charles Harper Webb

Superman, Old

He can still fly, and squeeze coal into diamonds, and see through walls and women's clothes; but sometimes, speeding through clouds, he loses control and tumbles like a spent bullet end over end, or forgets where he's going, and has to take a taxi home.

He lives alone—Clark Kent, retired reporter—but believes spies sneak into his room and steal his shoes.

Old *Daily Planets* heap up in his hall.

The Health Department calls about cockroaches. He shoves the inspector through a wall.

When Jimmy Olsen dies, then Perry White, he wants to die too. But Earth has no kryptonite.

Three knives shatter on his wrists. Eight bullets of ascending caliber ping off his skull.

He jumps in front of a train. It derails, killing fifty; he walks away.

His tantrums topple tall buildings. The SWAT Team sent for him retreats with casualties.

The CIA finds Lois in a nursing home. Kidneys shot and colon gone, she says she'll help.

A helicopter lowers her wheelchair into the rubble where Superman sleeps.

She leans down to stroke his cheek. "Superman? It's me."

He jerks upright, eyes baffled. "Old lady—who are you?"

"I'm your mother, Superman," she lies.

His brow softens. "I missed you, Mom."

"Do you remember Lois Lane?" she asks.

He scrunches up his face—still young and handsome as a boy's. "Kinda," he says. "She was pretty."

"Lex Luthor has her. Up there." Lois points at Cassiopeia, glittering. "Can you see her?"

Superman squints. "I don't know . . ."

She takes his hand, still strong as steel. "Lois needs you, Superman. You've got to save her."

"Lois," he whispers, and stands.

She straightens his cape.

"Who are you?" he asks.

"Your mother, Superman. Save Lois. Please."

"Save Louis," he says. Stretching hands above his head, he bends his knees.

"Fly, Clark," she says, then grips his cape, and lets his leap yank her up out of her wheelchair.

Her heart slows as the air thins. Then it stops, her hands relax, and she falls like the last booster of a rocket that, an instant later, starts tumbling end over end toward its home in the stars.

Bryan D. Dietrich

DRAWN TO MARVEL

Diagnosed diabetic the year I was born,
   You must begin with circles, some the size
my cousin taught me to live. How to let go
   of certain change, a dime, say, two quarters.
of a lit bottle rocket, pop the tarred, dark
   In the extremities, use even smaller ovals,
bubbles on days so hot the streets boiled, guide
   a geometry of diminishing returns.
go-carts, build robots. How to skate, stilt walk,
   As you move from one arc to the next,
clock a cropped horned toad with a rock, dodge that bright
   surprise yourself with lines, connecting
blood, what shot from its eyes. How to know a hero
   absence to absence until the frame
when you saw one, tri-colored, caped, omni-identitied.
   creates a trajectory of seeming
Late nights, lacklost in Lubbock, we'd saddle up the ghost
   action that almost looks like it could live.
cycle, thumb our way through Kung Fu, Daredevil,
   The hero you have begun—this stick figure
the man without fear, Doctor Fate, Tommy Tomorrow,
   fueled by long white, graphite, eraser stubble,
Spectre, Steel Sterling, man of steel, the New
   raggedy man made up of mostly empty
Gods, Kamandi, the last boy on earth.
   space—this imagined muscle vessel,
If it weren't for the diapers, ampoules of insulin
   well, he needs just that. Start with each
in the Frigidaire, you'd've never known. He lived
   oblique, with the beauty of the gut.
this way, in my memory, for years. Then suddenly
   Continue with the pecs, making sure
it's '82. They cut off his right leg. Dialysis begins
   to look for where they connect. Don't leave
seven years later. Three-hour hauls to the hospital,
   his breast heavy only, unable to support
three days a week, seven hours of recycling,
   itself. Deltoid, bi-, tricep, the curdled

new blood nearly every other day. The next year,

ripple of all you wish to appear,

paralytic. Dead from the chest down. Still,

as they say, ripped…all this complex anatomy

he can drive with hand controls, ride horses

may require help. Perhaps you should

with a special saddle, keep his family believing

consult a book. If not, stop now, return

by joking, popping wheelies in his chair.

where you started. Take off your clothes

Then, three years before the end, bed bruises, skin grafts,

look at yourself, see how we all fit together.

more than seven hundred stitches, arthritis, kidney

Bone, muscle, blood vessel, stubble, the subtle

infection, colostomy, the other leg.

breaks between one undiscovered region

A sore so deep it never heals. Later, the heart

and another. Finished? Time now for

attacks, two of them. And hands…gone. Eyes, gone.

the face, the hair, shadow on the brow, under toes,

Graduated drowning; his own humors. The day

other assorted endowments. Finally

before he dies, strangers from Tombstone come

the costume. What you've been waiting for.

to take him for a ride in a covered carriage.

This must be perfect, new, surprising,

It is April—month the poets call cruel, flower

able to expand in every direction. He's a symbol,

of the new millennium—when he finally says stop it,

don't forget. He must perform miracles, he must

stop,

be brave.

please,

Braver still when just

just turn off

standing. He must abandon

the machines

mere design, drawn to what marvel he was made for.

Becky Boyle

DARK

It starts in the tricolor acetate lithography
of a panel-blocked Gotham noir. You seek
to reverse that night in that alley: close walls,
a scream, two shots then blood. Pearls bursting
on the pavement—the bullets that started it all.

With a spiked cowl and scalloped wings, spurred gauntlets
and a utility belt toothed with knives sliced
in that kitschy animal shape. A crusade swept
under your cape like a cloak of night, a shadow cast,
your heart lies under onyx rubber and hooked stars.

A graphite mask beveled to your cheek—you despised
your fear so you slipped inside its pitch.
Art deco, bizarre science, lunatics, mobsters and ninjas—
from daguerreotyped skyscrapers under umber skies,
the city looks dirty on those eaves.

Nocturne of anarchy, with a slick snap you draw
your mantle with one impassioned fist, the crushing
clench of revenge—memory is so treacherous, so flighty—
guilt drops into ink-pools of anger, your drive
to do great or terrible things. Your growl to the night

leaves huge echoes in the sable caves of your mind.
Justice, a white beacon hisses to you in the sky.
Do they not know the batty blindness of right?
Apocalyptic wings grow heavy from decades
of use, of sketches and erasures, distorted faces

and buried names on rain-pelted graves.
A symbol, a hooded reaper of all this simple
filth drawn in straight lines across the page, you
know the achromatic tones of compassion, the real
ambiguous humanity of being good.

Anthony Frame

EVERYTHING I KNOW I LEARNED FROM SUPERHERO COMIC BOOKS

There's a football-sized hole in
the nuclear power plant

that's nestled on the outskirts of town.
I'm not worried; I know

a radiated body only grows stronger
and sometimes turns green.

In my head, I'm Batman, but
staring in the mirror, my eyes covered

by Coke-bottle glasses, even I
have to admit no amount of Jiu-Jitsu

will make me worthy of the cape
and cowl. I'd be lucky to sit

in Robin's sidecar so I'll definitely
need an atomic boost to become

heroic. Spider-Man looked like me
before the nuclear spider bite

and he had as much trouble fitting in
in his square-jawed world. But

I've watched enough 1950s movies
to know radiation poisoning

should have made the spider
a giant, forcing suburban throngs

to flee into cinematic history.
Still, there's always a hero, even if

he's too human for my tastes,
always on the lookout for the right

pretty girl, the best sunset
to conclude his epic. And anyway,

why should science be the remedy
for science? As if Bruce Banner

wouldn't need so many pairs of purple pants
if he could only use his physics degree

to decode himself. I'm happy
being ignorant of reality; no need

to think about *The Day After* or how
it made even Reagan worry about

nuclear strength. So give me that
radiated glow, those anatomically impossible

muscles ripped from our atomic
subconscious. I want tights stretched

as thin as my insecurities and a cape
that dances despite my skin-

and-bones physique. Saving the world
looks better after a trip to a tailor

with tight lips, but I'd rather not wear
a mask with eyeholes as Freudian mirrors.

Clark Kent gets to wear glasses
and have x-ray vision. All I want

is the power to clearly see
that symbol stretching across my heart.

Ryan G. Van Cleave

HE WHO DRAWS SUPERMAN

must take particular care with the cape,
which is not the single-purposed
red of oblivion, but an unethereal
backbone that hoists up the world—
the type of dahlia manteau which makes
crooks draw terror up to their chins.

His pupils, too, absolutely must be
anonymous, flawless black. No Clark
Kent here; they've got to be unamazed!
Let Superman's gaze be two blue
thuds in Lake Erie, not the oily brown
of a sludge-sifter journalist for the *Planet*.

He who draws Superman must be
obsessed by the desert, the wide-open
places of this world that freeze at night
into the ice palace at the North Pole.
He must have a voice in his head,
an echo in that vast cathedral of the skull.

Most importantly, every line, each
erasure must be in a firm belief that
Supreme Intelligence exists. Screw
kryptonite. Forget Lex Luthor.
What makes him super is the dot
of theology, the footprint of the divine,

the extra unnoticed line—his dour grin.

Joey Nicoletti

WHAT I LEARNED FROM JOHN ROMITA, SR.

Learning to draw is learning to see.

Start by using bits of plaster

from torn-down buildings

as chalk, then sketch

the Statue of Liberty

on your city street.

One's take on Spider-Man

is another's on pomodoro sauce:

ample, robust, developed

after countless attempts and hours

of practice, long after

Christoforo Colombo's name

was Anglicized; long after

Christopher Columbus brought

the tomato back

from the New World; long after

my family migrated from Italia to America.

Let your children sit on your lap

while you work:

humans, cats, and dogs alike.

Comic books can be good for you,

like a glass of red wine every day;

like the prosciutto, fig, and arugula salad

as the first course of Sunday dinner

at my parents' house.

Look sharp. Don't be afraid

of muscular men, shapely blondes,

redheads or green goblins. Be yourself,

whether you draw protagonists

with strong chins, or stars

in tonight's sky, soaking

through storm clouds,

like an archenemy's glasses.

Christi Krug

PENCIL BOY

My brother has pencils of all shapes and sizes in his headquarters. His desk is old-fashioned, scratched up with names and stuck under the seat with gum leavings, cold smooth lumps of Wrigley's from kids already grown up somewhere, already uncles and grandparents. There's an inkwell, a dark airhole, and sitting crooked on top is a cottage cheese container with my brother's pencils. He saves them. He sharpens them down to the nubs.

My brother erases, making rubbery pink and gray worms that wriggle when brushed away. His headquarters should be filled with rubbery pink and gray worms. It isn't.

When an eraser wears down to the metal, the gold thin band becomes an empty crown, and the next time you erase, it scratches the paper. This doesn't happen to my brother.

My brother is Superhero of the Short, Sharp Pencil. He never runs out of pencils. His eraser knows no end. He uses the shortest of his sharp pencils and writes the name given him by our father, who used to be alive. He writes the name tiny. Like the writing on a toy. Like the words in Marvel Comics, hard to see. My brother's printing is careful, like someone who is shrinking and may turn invisible because of the secret formula of a mad scientist. In all the stories, the superhero used to be an ordinary person until a terrible accident happened. A chemical thing or freaky weather or almost dying. The superhero mutates because of the terrible accident, and gets filled with a sense of responsibility to use his powers for the betterment of mankind.

My brother's pencil sharpener, a chamber of power, goes *grnn, grrn, grrn*. He draws cartoons. He reads *Scientific American*, does math. Tiny pencils get thinner. He is not afraid of numbers, those skinny smart things without faces. His own face he does not show. When the doorbell rings, he stays in his headquarters until whoever it is goes away.

All through the rooms, we leave dishes and socks under beds and behind chairs. Not so, in my brother's headquarters. The air smells like pencil shavings and feels like a white paper echo, clean and far away.

Our uncles and grandparents say he is man of the house now, but still
a very strange boy. Why does he stay behind closed doors? Why did he
strike his cousin without warning, until the blood streamed down her face?

Nobody understands science like my brother, Superhero of the Short,
Sharp Pencil. If a disastrous chemical explosion unleashed his alter ego, he
would understand about it. Even if everyone thought he was crazy. That
is the way with superheroes. Someone has to save mankind from being
destroyed.

Charles Hatfield

GREETINGS, CULTURE LOVERS!

> *Seizing the opportunity for mischief, Stanley...inscribed four fateful*
> *words on the ceiling—"Stan Lee is God." That was the first known use of*
> *this famous pseudonym.*
> > —Raphael & Spurgeon, *Stan Lee and the Rise and Fall of the*
> > *American Comic Book (2003)*

Hard not to admire it
When it comes at you so nakedly,
This craft of trumpeting oneself, of
Horn-tooting, branding, memyselfandaye—

Dig his antic, capering Self, smiling larger than life,
Giving up a bit of his boundless whatever to
Jolt us into faith:

Taskmaster, impresario, front-facer,
Imprimatur for thousands of pencil-and-paper dreams,
He who reined in comets, shaping,
Captioning, grounding so many zero-gee fantasies

(so much skywriting! born of so many
down-to-earth drawing boards,
this in itself a marvel,
month-to-month and
paycheck-to-paycheck,
far in fact from his fraternal mythic Bullpen),

and packaging, Barnumizing, glossing all,

Over years the public face
Of imagination unleashed, original energy, and all that—

Lo, he doth bestride the four-color earth like a living colossus,
Higher, higher still, perennially young,
Long retired, never-retiring
   (playing extra in his own world),
Years on from doing anything, really, but

Still, as ever, giving us, ourselves,
      back to ourselves, in small packages.

Ringmaster, totem, smiling one,
Rallying the happy few,
we band of readers, initiates, ingrates and fans,
some miffed, maybe, to have been so long entranced,
But all of us, just the same,

All of us pilgrims.

Chris Gavaler

PARAGON COMICS

1.

An aunt yanks Dotty's arm straight as they bustle toward a steamship belching clouds from its smokestack. The woman's head but not her words are out of frame: "Hurry up, dear. Have to get you safe." Dotty's head is turned, gaze caught in the upchurned dirt of the blockaded street. Cracks in the shattered asphalt zigzag under her tiny boots, the round crater edge almost a straight line. Next panel from the crater bottom, little Dotty peering down, framed by the ambiguous green of the yet unseen flower. The stem towers higher than the bombed-out storefronts slouching behind her. The page is gray-browns and brown-grays, except for that one unearthly sprout of color, more Dali than Kirby. Of course Dotty tugs her hand free from the woman's grip, doesn't notice the thinly inked hum of bombers as she scampers bare-kneed into the pit, the woman's "Dotty!" drawn over by the whirring black letters of an air raid siren. What matters are the unfolding petals. The impossible glow of that opening mouth, brighter than the scribbled explosions of the street above. Dotty's hand is enormous, its pink closing around her prize.

2.

Flip the page and there's Dotty under the white of her hospital sheet, nursing uniforms plodding out of panel. The aunt is absent. We're not told that Dotty's disobedient leap saved her life. A plucked miracle. She is looking at her clenched hand, fingers opening petal-like. They're empty. The flower is gone. But lean closer, look at those marks on her palm, a kind of scar, a tattoo burned into the pink, only brighter, a sprout of color. Later issues, it's a shrunken version of the stylized "P" on every cover. By No. 4, the frills and lightning-jagged stem slip into simplicity, offspring of repetition and deadlines. But how amorphous this original rendering, Dotty's first glimpse of the scar that transforms her.

3.

"Dotty," the voices call. "Can you hear us?" The alien scientists sport dress-length lab coats and Buck Rogers helmets. Their panel edges are squiggly with interdimensional distortion. Dotty can't see them, but her eyes contract to a pair of dot-pricked circles of surprise. She doesn't answer, not at first. She's back at school, crammed into a row of desks, copying the tiny letters a teacher spells at the distant chalkboard—like the aunt's, the

teacher's head is out of frame—but later, alone on the playground, the
pendulums of children's swings far beyond her shoulder, Dotty whispers:
Who are you, where are you radioing from, how can I get there? The answer is in
the palm of her hand. "Clap," they tell her. Clap one tattooed hand against
the naked other and she will never be the same little girl again.

4.

Anyone could have plucked the fake flower, been implanted with its
circuitry. It's not clear whether the probe was engineered for a girl's
curiosity, if those Dimension P scientists knew who they were trapping.
Dotty doesn't need a ring to engage her, no magic words to alter her. Why
settle for a skin-tight leotard under your skirt suit, when you can keep a
whole man inside your body? It's her first time, but Dotty flings herself
into the path of the runaway truck hurtling toward the stalled school bus.
A clap of lightning and from her quivering smoke lines her savior blooms,
bare-chested but for his P-branded pectorals. The sandals and loin cloth are
a space-aged Roman's, the physique Johnny Weissmuller's. "Behold!" his
talk bubble roars. "The mighty Paragon will save you now!"

5.

Comic books only give the perpetual middle, endless foreplay, then
cancellation mid-story, no climax. *Paragon* froze at No. 20. A painted ship
upon a painted sea. Time should be a striptease, a drumroll ending with
a cymbal-flutter of the final, reveal-all stitch of cloth. The old pulp heroes,
they had fiancés, lady friends willing to peek under the mask, to tug it all
off. Time didn't jilt you bimonthly, didn't dangle Lois lane lip-pursed on
your window ledge as her ubervirgin swoops away. For Dotty, a world
without closure is a life without puberty, the ultimate prophylactic. When
she swaps dimensions with Paragon, her tomboy body whisks away to a
stasis tube in the Cathedral of Science. She watches from a thought bubble
over her hero's head, cratered in the present tense. Safe forever. She never
gets any action. Dotty is twelve. Dotty will always be twelve. Even after
the war. Even now. A forgotten Golden Ager lapsed into public domain.
When I scissored open the package, her pages were brittle and rust-stained
around the staples, but mostly intact. It's best to turn them with the palms
of both hands.

Jessie Carty

DRAWN TO HEROES

Mom always purchased the leftover comics
at the end of the month from Woodard's Drug.

I was in love with too many of them
to pick a favorite. I'd read anything.

I wanted to look like Dazzler with her blonde hair
and roller skates or

at least I thought I could be Betty with her tomboyish charm.
I was drawn to the scrappy

heroes like the unsung Power Pack while my brother
championed the usual Spider Men and Batboys

as if he hoped he'd wake one day
having been bitten

by a radioactive moth or to have suddenly discovered
he was actually adopted

and that his real parents left him all their wealth
along with

a hermit crab shell the size of Manhattan
that could be his fortress

because we thought everything large
was the size of Manhattan.

Robert Avery

SUPERHEROES

All morning he draws and draws,
crumpling one image after another,
and, leaning over, I see it's Batman—

horned head, stick arms with stick fingers
stretched out in welcome, or to poke
the cynical Riddler to his knees;

the feet lucky 7's upside-down;
and a great blank cape behind
like a flag of the boy's faith.

The figure doesn't look like a real person—
like me, for instance.
One day he'll realize that, and

perhaps refuse my arms held out.
But right now he asks me to fly with him,
and of course I say yes, and clip

two checkered dishtowels to our shirts,
and he goes running around the house,
and occasionally glances back—

at his cape billowing out, or because
he doesn't hear my loyal step
behind. But I'm there, still,

if half-unseen—defending that state
one only grasps in exile—before
mere rags and clearly fallible men.

Tim Hunt

POEM THOUGHT MAYBE

he should learn to draw. There was,
He sensed, a market niche for a super
Hero comic, not something weird,

Not Spider-Poem or X-Poems or Trans-
Poemers, but something more clean cut,
Without all the mutant cross-dressing

Or genetic mash-up. Perhaps
Batpoem and Robin! They could have
A super Poemmobile, made entirely

Out of nifty allusions, something sleek
And super-modernist. And a Poem
Cave! With lots of high tech gear—secret

Meters and stanza forms that could
Be used to cleanse the grime of prosaic
Crime! And a canny but doting

Butler named J. Alfred. And Batpoem
Could have a Double Identity! Socialite
Denotation by day, Connotation by night—

A cape with radiating pixels of gray innuendo.
Poem could easily imagine the villains:
Heroic Couplet, for sure, and maybe the

Word Hoarder, perhaps even Pathetic
Fallacy. But maybe even that was
Too weird. Maybe it should be Superpoem,

A hero who could fly in the light,
His bright blue spandex impervious
To all ambiguity. That, Poem thought,

Was beyond weird.

Ned Balbo

FOR JACOB KURTZBERG
Better known as Jack Kirby (1917-1993)

Nothing beyond his power, in Mineola,
drawing furiously, the artist Jacob,
"Jack" to friends and fans, finds one idea
compels him, hurtling, through every job—

for money, sure, but also (lit cigar stub
trailing smoke) for love: he knows his genre
offers myth, and heroes need a problem
that will test their powers. In Mineola,

working from home (postwar suburbia),
an East Side kid, Jack punched his way past trouble,
gave the world Captain America,
and more: the pantheon of heroes Jacob

draws for Marvel now. Aye, there's the rub
(eraser-shreds brushed back, tabula rasa
of the next page waiting): credit-grabbing
wordsmith Stan will think this new idea

is his alone; still, pages fill the sofa,
ready for the shoot. No time for "grub"—
Jack's on a mission, as at Omaha
ten days after the landing, when the job

eclipsed, by far, some petty contract's quota.
But what foe must his quartet face and clobber?
—*A silver angel falls, his gleaming aura*
crackling as he wakes in fiery rubble,
nothing beyond his power.

Note: Information on the life and career of comics giant Jack Kirby is drawn from *The Comics Journal Library, Volume One: Jack Kirby* (Fantagraphics Books: Seattle, WA: 2002), especially "Interview I: 'There is something stupid in violence as violence'" (conducted by Mark Hebert) and "Interview II: 'I created an army of characters, and now my connection with them is lost'" (conducted by Tim Skelly).

Kirby co-created Captain America with Joe Simon prior to the U.S. entry into WWII. Kirby's collaborator and editor during the 1960s (and co-creator of the Marvel Universe) was Stan Lee. The "fallen angel" is the Silver Surfer, herald of world-devouring Galactus.

Albert Goldbarth

POWERS

Whizzer, The Top, Phantasmo. . . . They come back sometimes,
now that my father comes back
sometimes. With their lightningbolts sewn
the size of dinner utensils across their chests, with their capes
rayed out, with their blue lamé boots. And he. . . ? It's
hazy, usually; he's a part of that haze. It talcs
his early-morning stubble, it muffles the worry
love so often set like candles in his eyes. And: "Albie . . ."/then
that smile meant kindly, but also to say it came from some source
wiser than mine/". . . all this reading is fine. But there's a
real world." It wasn't The Streak. It wasn't Mistress Miracle.
With their antigravity belts, their bellcurve muscles.
Night. One lamp. While he read every scrap of fiscal scribble
that said the rent couldn't be met, and in the darkness
tried to fight that vague opponent with every poor
persuasive scrappy peddler's stratagem he had, I read
by flashlight under the covers: City Hall was being burgled
of its Gems of the World display, and Captain Invincible faced
a Mineral Ray (that already turned two bank guards and a porter
into clumsily rendered crystalline statues) jauntily,
his wisecracks by themselves could make a "mobster" or
that dreaded gorillaish creature in a double-breasted suit,
a mobster's "goon," collapse in the ultimate cowardly self-exposure
of "crooks" and "scoundrels" everywhere. The Dynamo
could will himself into a wielder of electrical jolts, and even
invaders from Alpha-10 were vanquished. Smasheroo's
special power was fists "with the force of entire armies."
Flamegirl was . . . well, flames. And flying,
almost all of them, blazoned on sky—a banner, an imperative
above our muddling lunch-and-shrubbery days.
With their "secret identities": Spectral Boy, who looks like someone's
winter breath (and so can enter "criminal hideouts" through keyholes,
etc.) is "in reality" Matt Poindexter, polo-playing dandy;
The Silver Comet, whose speed is legendary and leaves
small silver smudges on the page as he near-invisibly zips by, is
ironically wheelchair-bound and Army-rejected
high school student and chemistry ace Lane Barker;
The Rocket Avenger parks cars; Celestia is a bosomy

ill-paid secretary. It could happen—couldn't it?—
to me: the thick clouds part as neat as prom-night hair
and a nacreous flask of Planet Nineteen's "wizard elixir" be
beamed down to my bedside: I would wake reciting
a Pledge Against Evil, and set to work designing whatever
emerald star or halo'd eye would be incised on my visor, it
could happen, right?—I wasn't Me but
an inchoate One of Them. With their Wave Transmitter Wristlets,
with their wands, their auras, their cowls. The Insect Master.
Blockbuster. Astro Man. Miss Mystery. Gold Bolt. Solaris. . . .
They come back to me now, they ring the bedroom air sometimes
like midges at the one watt of my consciousness, and sleep
is entered with this faint token of sentinel benignity upon me.
Maybe because sleep also
isn't what my father called the "real world." And
he . . . ? Dead
now, with his stone, with his annual candle, my father is
also a fiction. And so he appears
with their right to appear, from the kingdom of the impossible,
he appears in their midst, with Doctor Justice,
The Genie, The Leopardess, Meteor Man . . . he steps out
from that powerpacked crowd, he's thrown his factory-outlet jacket
sloppily over his shoulders, it's late, so dark now, and
he's worried about me. Someone may as well be. I'm
in pieces over some new vexation: hopeless in the drizzle,
perhaps, a flashlight clamped abobble in my mouth, and trying to find
          whatever
damage in the mysterious shrieks and greaseways of an engine
bucked me ditchside in the wee hours; or, with equal befuddlement,
staring damp-eyed at the equally damaged wants and generosities
awhirr in the human heart. And: "Albie . . ." / then that very
gentle yet censorious shake of the head / ". . . how many times
have I told you? Be patient. Never force your tools or materials.
Don't give up." At moments like this, that his blood
pumps though me, his blood is half of what actually made me, seems
as wondrous as Bob Frank "deep in the jungles of Africa"
dying of fever and being saved by—positively
thriving on—a transfusion of mongoose blood.

This was in 1941, in *USA Comics*; Frank returned to New York
as the Whizzer—superfast, in an outfit
the yellow of mariners' slickers. And Triphammer.
Ghost King. The Scarlet Guardian. Eagleman. Magic Scarab. The Wraith.
With their domino masks or their gladiatorial helmets.
The Mighty Elasto. Lady Radiant. Space Devil. Reptile Boy.
With their various signs of legitimacy: their pharaonic rings,
atomic lariats, stun guns, mystic arrows, tridents, with
such amulets as hinge the Earth and Heavens into symbiotic grace.
The Invoker: I remember, he kept two planets at peace. And Hydro-Man:
could turn to water (a dubious strength, I always thought) and once
he conducted a current that fried some miscreant, so rescued
a willowy flibbertigibbet princess. And Panther Woman: her golden claws
and sinuous inky tail were all the good that (successfully) stood between
a scientist "bent on enslaving the world to his crazed whims" and
the populace of "Center City," the first place on his list. And
Whizzer . . . I remember, once, Whizzer was . . . I put down the page.
The knocking. The landlady. He was shaking
in front of her. She filled the door. He had to explain
the doctor cost extra money this month, and he worked all week
on double shifts, he really did, but this one time
we didn't have the rent, we'd be late, he was fighting back crying,
who'd never had to say such a thing before to such a person,
I remember: he said it straight to her face,
the one good pair of suit pants keeping its crease in the closet
cried but he didn't, the long day's wadded-up tissues cried out,
and the bar sign blinking pinkly across the street,
the horseshoes of dust that collect on the house slippers under the bed,
The Little Taxi That Hurried and *Scuffy the Tugboat*, that sorrily stained
lame angelwing of an ironing board, the ashtrays and the aspirin,
everything yielded up its softness then,
the carpet was green and black, the light was ruthless,
his voice never broke and his gaze never shifted although
the universe did, because we would be one week late, there! he said it,
he said it clearly, to her and to everyone,
spent, and heroic.

DRAWN

TO MARVEL

POEMS FROM THE COMIC BOOKS

EDITED BY BRYAN D. DIETRICH AND MARTA FERGUSON

Alternate Cover by Matt Cresswell

MINOR
ARCANA
PRESS

ISSUE X
VOLUME X

Alternate Cover by Mel Li

ACKNOWLEDGMENTS

Sherman Alexie. The excerpt from Sherman Alexie's "Totem Sonnets" from THE SUMMER OF THE BLACK WIDOWS. Hanging Loose Press. Copyright © 1996 by Sherman Alexie. Reprinted by permission of Hanging Loose Press.

Celia Lisset Alvarez. "Superman Confronts Me About Dinner" and "Wonder Woman Goes Through Menopause." Printed by permission of the author.

Rae Armantrout. "Previews" from VERSED by Rae Armantrout. Wesleyan University Press. Copyright © 2009 by Rae Armantrout. Reprinted by permission of Wesleyan University Press.

Michael Arnzen. "The Gentlest Monster" and "Proverbs for Monsters" from PROVERBS FOR MONSTERS by Michael A. Arnzen. Dark Regions Press, 2007. Copyright © 2007 by Michael Arnzen. Reprinted by permission of the author. "Sister Superman" printed by permission of the author.

John Ashbery. "Farm Implements and Rutabagas in a Landscape" from THE DOUBLE DREAM OF SPRING by John Ashbery. Copyright © 1966, 1970 by John Ashbery. Reprinted by permission of Georges Borchardt, Inc., on behalf of the author.

Robert Avery. "Superheroes." Printed by permission of the author.

Ned Balbo. "The Crimefighter's Apprentice" from THE TRIALS OF EDGAR POE AND OTHER POEMS by Ned Balbo. Copyright © 2010 by Ned Balbo. Reprinted by permission of Story Line Press. "For Jacob Kurtzberg" originally appeared in *Archaeopteryx*. Reprinted by permission of the author. "Flash of Two Worlds" printed by permission of the author.

Tony Barnstone. "The Blowfly Thing" and "The Human Torch." Printed by permission of the author.

Anne Bean. "The Decomposition of Alec Holland." Printed by permission of the author.

Tara Betts. "Oya Invites Storm to Tea" originally appeared in *Mythium*, Issue #1 in Fall 2009. Reprinted by permission of the author.

Bruce Boston. "Curse of the Superhero's Wife" by Bruce Boston from THE COMPLETE ACCURSED WIVES. Talisman/Dark Regions. Copyright © 2000 by Bruce Boston. Reprinted by permission of the author.

Becky Boyle. "Dark." Printed by permission of the author.

Ryan Bradley. "Haikus from Supervillains to the People They Love" and "Our Love." Printed by permission of the author.

Andrew Scott Browers. "Please Don't Call Me Clark." Printed by permission of the author.

Kurt Brown. "The Heap" provided by the Estate of Kurt Brown. Reprinted by permission of Laure-Anne Bosselaar, literary executor.

John F. Buckley & Martin Ott. "With This Ring." Printed by permission of the authors.

Chris Bullard. "Sidekick." Printed by permission of the author.

Stephen Burt. "Little Lament for the Legion of Super-Heroes" from BELMONT. Copyright © 2013 by Stephen Burt. "Self-Portrait as Kitty Pryde" and "Scenes from Next Week's

George Longenecker. "Superboy" originally appeared in *Dos Passos Review*. Reprinted by permission of the author.

David Lunde. "Superman *Inoxydable*" by David Lunde originally appeared in *Asimov's Science Fiction*. Reprinted by permission of the author.

Kathryn Howd Machan. "No, Superman Was Not the Only One" from BELLY WORDS. Sometimes Y Publications. Copyright © 1994 by Kathryn Howd Machan. Reprinted by permission of the author.

Amy MacLennan. "Tinfoil and Twisty Ties." Printed by permission of the author.

Harry Man. "J. Jonah Jameson." Printed by permission of the author.

Michael Martone. "The Sex Life of the Fantastic Four" by Michael Martone from FOUR FOR A QUARTER: FICTIONS. Fiction Collective 2 (FC₂)/University of Alabama Press. Copyright © 2011 by Michael Martone. Reprinted by permission of the author.

Adrian Matejka. "America's First and Foremost Black Superstar", from MIXOLOGY by Adrian Matejka, copyright © 2009 by Adrian Matejka. Used by permission of Penguin, a division of Penguin Group (USA) LLC.

Laurel Maury. "Love Song for Marvin the Martian." Printed by permission of the author.

Jason McCall. "Superman Watches Lois Lane Pull Weeds" originally appeared in Story's debut issue, Spring 2014 (http://www.storymagazine.org). Reprinted by permission of the author. "Sidekick Funeral: Jason Todd" and "Why the Sentry Doesn't Write Love Poems" printed by permission of the author.

John McCarthy. "Between Land and Sea." Printed by permission of the author.

Raymond McDaniel. "Colossal Boy Loves Shrinking Violet," "The Menace of Dream Girl," and "The Persistence of Espionage" from SPECIAL POWERS AND ABILITIES. Copyright © 2013 by Raymond McDaniel. Reprinted with the permission of The Permissions Company, Inc., on behalf of Coffee House Press, www.coffeehousepress.org.

Campbell McGrath. "Hunger" from ROAD ATLAS: PROSE AND OTHER POEMS. Ecco/HarperCollins. Copyright © 1999 by Campbell McGrath. Reprinted by permission of Ecco/HarperCollins, Hopewell, NJ 08525.

Wesley McNair. "The Thugs of Old Comics." Printed by permission of the author.

Oscar McNary. "Neil" from SARAN WRAP LEISURE SUIT. Copyright © 2011 by Oscar McNary. Reprinted by permission of the author.

Kelly McQuain. "Vampirella." Printed by permission of the author.

P. Andrew Miller. "Aquaman" originally appeared in *Eye to the Telescope*. Reprinted by permission of the author. "Zatanna's Haiku" and "Aquaman" printed by permission of the author.

Eric Morago. "Thor Loses His Hammer" from WHAT WE ACHE FOR. Moon Tide Press. Copyright © 2010 by Eric Morago. Reprinted by permission of Moon Tide Press.

Jason Mott. "A Song for Healers" and "A Dream Remembered Two Days After My Father Enters Hospice" from ...HIDE BEHIND ME... Main Street Rag. Copyright © 2011 by Jason Mott. Reprinted by permission of the author. "An Open Letter to Up and Coming World-Savers" printed by permission of the author.

INDEX BY AUTHOR

N

O

P

R

S

ALSO AVAILABLE FROM MINOR ARCANA PRESS...

Skin Job
by Evan J. Peterson

Zebra Feathers
by Morris Stegosaurus

Gay City 5: Ghosts in Gaslight, Monsters in Steam
edited by Vincent Kovar & Evan J. Peterson
in partnership with the Gay City Health Project

FORTHCOMING FROM MINOR ARCANA PRESS...

Shufflepoems
by Lydia Swartz
a deck of shuffleable poetry

Monster Fancy
a literary magazine for the discerning monster enthusiast

WWW.MINORARCANAPRESS.COM

Minor Arcana Press Logo designed and painted by Sergio Coya.